History
TODAY

Thomas Bilney
Forgotten Reformer

Stuart Fisher

DayOne

© Day One Publications 2022

ISBN 978-1-84625-738-4

British Library Cataloguing in Publication Data available

Published by Day One Publications
Ryelands Road, Leominster, HR6 8NZ
Telephone 01568 613 740 FAX 01568 611 473
email—sales@dayone.co.uk
website—www.dayone.co.uk

Cover design by Kathryn Chedgzoy
Printed by 4edge

To Lizzie my loving wife,
best friend and helper.

Endorsements

Stuart Fisher writes with an historian's head and a preacher's heart in providing us with this fascinating biography of a forgotten hero from church history. But this book is not just for preachers. Thomas Bilney's life provides encouragement for us all in days where there is a growing hostility towards the gospel. We all will identify with the struggles of 'Little Bilney' but let us pray we too will have the impact he had upon the nation he loved and served so well.'

Mike Mellor, Pastor, evangelist and author of several Day One Publications

Thomas Bilney, though timid, was the tinderbox that God used to spark the Reformation in England! It thrilled my heart to read about how God chose a 'little' man for such lofty purposes and caused me to cry out that he would do it again in our own day. A soul-stirring, deeply captivating read from cover to cover!

Jimmy Hill, Pastor of Moordown Baptist Church, Bournemouth

Contents

Preface

In Ecclesiastes 11:1 (ESV), we are told to 'cast your bread upon the waters, for you will find it after many days.' Way back in 1997, I was sitting in the garden on a sunny day, absorbed in a book on the English Reformation. I noticed how often the name, Thomas Bilney, cropped up. So many books on the Reformation quoted him, especially in reference to Hugh Latimer, yet there seemed to be little information about him. I started to make notes, searching out every scrap of information that I could lay hands on. The result was a short article on Bilney. I then sent this off to The *Evangelical Times* (*ET*), in the hope that they may be interested. Roger Fay and Edgar Andrews kindly encouraged me by agreeing to print the article, which appeared in the February 1998 edition of the paper (little did I know that years later Roger would become my youngest son's father-in-law!). It was republished in *ET* in 2014.

Fast forward to the year 2018 and I was contacted by Colin Hart of the Christian Institute. They were preparing a series of lectures on key English Reformers and it had been suggested by Dr Richard Turnbull that I be contacted with the possibility of speaking on Bilney at the conference in Newcastle. I agreed to this, giving me the stimulus to research further. I was surprised to find so little written about Bilney. *Foxe's Book of Martyrs* was the main source along with Marcus Loane's most helpful update in his *Masters of the English Reformation*, which gave Bilney equal footing with other luminaries of the English Reformation. The lecture was kindly received and among the questions at the end was why I had not written a book on Bilney. That was a challenge I took home with me. During the dark clouds of Covid-19, I took the opportunity to do more research and eventually a manuscript was written, which was accepted for publication. It was a long but exciting process, only made possible by the support and encouragement of others.

I would like to thank Roger and Edgar for first nurturing the seed; Dr Richard Turnbull and Colin Hart in taking the risk with an unknown speaker; Mark Roberts and the Day One team for agreeing to publish the book; and Mike Mellor and Jimmy Hill for being such great encouragers. But, above all, my wife Lizzie who did the proofreading, endured my ups and downs in bringing the book to completion and for never losing faith in me.

So, I pray this little book will honour a forgotten hero but, more than that, the God he served. To God be all the glory.

Stuart Fisher

Timeline of Bilney's life

1495		Born in Norfolk
1510		Enters Trinity Hall Cambridge
1519		Ordained a priest
1519		Converted while reading Erasmus's New Testament
1520		Bachelor of Law & Fellow of Trinity Hall
1524		Bilney's 'confession' to Latimer
1525	**July**	Bilney is licenced to preach further afield
1527		Bilney & Latimer reprimanded by Wolsey
1527	**Spring**	Bilney & Arthur preaching tour
1527	**November**	Summoned to London before Wolsey
1527	**December**	Bilney recants
1528		Bilney in prison
1531		Recommences preaching in Norfolk
1531		Bilney dies at Lollards Pit, Norwich.

Figure 1: Thomas Bilney

Introduction – why forgotten?

C hurch history is a great love of mine. Seeing God's hand in every event is both instructive and encouraging. To know that He is in control of absolutely everything. One of the most exciting periods of church history is the Reformation, when God breaks through to restore His Church from the ages of darkness, error and superstition. While studying the English Reformation, I constantly came across the name, Thomas Bilney. What puzzled me was that in most of the general histories, with the outstanding exception of *Foxes Acts and Monuments*, he was little more than a footnote, or in some, a few pages. In biographies of his more illustrious contemporary, Latimer, he fares a little better. Probably, the one honourable exception is Marcus Loane's, *Masters of the English Reformation*, which at least gives a good account of the man along with other more famous Reformers. It is my contention that he was not a minor background figure among the great but a true hero in his own right and worthy of greater recognition. Bilney was the first to discover and read Erasmus's New Testament text in England, the man who led the great Latimer to faith in Christ and the first in the Reformation period to be martyred for his faith. These facts alone should merit Bilney a higher position than he now occupies and yet there are still, even today, scant resources about such a worthy man. So, what is the reason for this neglect? It is difficult to be certain but there are several possibilities. One reason might be that Bilney did actually recant his faith, albeit briefly, and for some, maybe, that was a good enough reason for putting him on the back shelf.

Another possibility is the difficulty in pigeonholing Bilney as a 'Classic Reformer'. In the strictest sense he was not a reformer, as we now understand the term, but he was more a bridge between older Lollard dissenters[1] and Reformers as we now know them today. I hope to consider his complex character later in the book, challenge these views and give him the greater respect that I believe he deserves. This led me to the subtitle, 'Forgotten Reformer'.

For some years, I have been researching, when time allows, on the life of Bilney, and have at last put together a small biography. I have kept assiduously to the facts available, but also tried to write in a way that is hopefully appealing to a wider audience. My desire is that this study might help bring the man from out of the shadows into a more prominent light—one I believe he deserves—and that the name of Thomas Bilney, so long forgotten, might again be known and honoured.

Notes

1 Lollardy was a nickname given to earlier 14th-Century reformers— followers of John Wycliffe.

1 Student days

Here is a trustworthy saying that deserves full acceptance: Christ Jesus came into the world to save sinners—of whom I am the worst (1 Timothy 1:15).

THE FORBIDDEN BOOK!

A small, heavily concealed figure grabbed the package and handed over the amount required. With the precious bundle carefully hidden under his cloak, he left the house, giving furtive glances in both directions. He passed, ghostlike through cobbled courtyards and up several steps, only pausing when in front of an archway to a small hall. A final glance and a brisk walk up a staircase took him to the safety of a familiar door. With trembling hands, he fumbled to put a key in the lock. Finally, inside, he slammed the door shut, locking and bolting it, then leant against the heavy frame to

Figure 2: Trinity Hall, Cambridge

steady himself. Perspiring, and with heart pounding, he made his way to a rough wooden chair. The remains of a fire smouldered in the grate, giving little warmth to the cheerless room. He sat down heavily, shivering, partly from fear and partly from cold. Dropping the package to his knees, he cautiously removed the papers, then froze as he heard voices outside. Students passing, their voices in high spirits, in anticipation of a night of revelry, as they clambered down the stairs. As the noise died, he returned to his precious treasure. On his knees lay the cause of his fear—a book, a forbidden book. He traced his finger over the embossed words, 'Novum Testamentum'. A further pause to pull a small table nearer, bearing the remains of a well-used candle. Quickly lit, he held the candle near while turning slowly the crisp pages of the book. Excitement overtaking his fear, he turned the pages more rapidly, his heart beating wildly. Then his eyes fell on a text that seemed to jump out at him:

> Here is a trustworthy saying that deserves full acceptance: Christ Jesus came into the world to save sinners—of whom I am the worst.

As he reread the precious words of 1 Timothy 1:15, light flooded into his soul. He read and reread those words, scarcely believing what was happening. This was the truth he had been longing to hear. A Saviour who had come to save sinners like him. His burden had gone he had found a Saviour. The young scholar, Thomas Bilney, would never be the same.

Young Bilney

Nine years earlier, in 1510, a slightly built, fresh-faced country boy jumped down from the wagon. He brushed himself down and placed a large, leather bag by his feet. As the horses pulled away to the drivers shout, so young Thomas Bilney stood in wonder, gazing up at the imposing buildings. Picking up his bag, Bilney, still only 15 years old, walked awkwardly towards the main gates. Small knots of gowned men pushed past him, oblivious to his existence. Small in stature and of a nervous disposition, Bilney felt overawed by this strange new world. He was about to enter the most significant stage in his young life. As his eyes scanned unfamiliar surroundings with the noise and bustle, he felt an overwhelming desire to withdraw—a longing to return home. Yet this was his new home, his calling. He was aware too of the high expectations of his family: their pride in his entering Cambridge University. Not many from his background would have that chance. Bilney had done well at school and was about to prepare for a future career in Law. If he kept his head down, worked hard and abided by the rules, life promised a rich reward.

Little is known of Bilney's background, records being scarce. The general opinion is that Bilney was born in 1495 in Norfolk. There is some speculation that he may have been born in Norwich or even, possibly East Bilney itself. It seems that the surname Bilney is most likely derived from the name of the village, East Bilney, Norfolk. Although East Bilney does not appear in the Domesday book, it has an ancient standing, being split between the Earl Warren of Gressendale and the Bishops of Norwich and Elmham. The name, 'Bil', derives from the tribal name, 'Billinger', and 'ey', meaning isle. The later probably refers to the fact that the Village of Bilney was originally an island surrounded by the river Nar.

The view that Thomas Bilney was born in or around this area is probably due to a story that some ashes were found in an urn in the churchyard of St Mary's, the local church where Bilney's ashes were

Figure 3: The image of Thomas Bilney in the window of St Mary's Church

put after his martyrdom. As the church was dedicated to the Assumption of the Virgin Mary, it would be an irony since one of the charges against Bilney was his casting doubt on the veneration of the Virgin![1]

He is certainly remembered as a significant figure in the area, even having his memory perpetuated in windows,[2] though there is no conclusive evidence that he was born there.

The Church now standing there is an almost complete reconstruction from the nineteenth century—the original only being remembered by a drawing (See Fig 4).

Entering Cambridge at such a young age may seem strange to us but, in those days, it was not so unusual. A century earlier, it would have been quite common. Even in Bilney's time, while less common, it was still not considered unusual. Bilney must have shown considerable promise to have even been chosen and must have had an aptitude for student life. He enrolled at Trinity Hall, the fifth-oldest college of Cambridge, founded in 1350 by William Bateman, Bishop of Norwich.

Historically, Trinity Hall had been set up for the specific purpose of preparing men for service in the Church as ecclesiastical lawyers. Both a study of Church (canon) law and civil law was therefore necessary. It seems that there were two courses open to the students. One would be to pursue a career in civil law or the other to be in canon law and serve the Church.[3]

Bilney, being a Norfolk man, would have been naturally drawn to this College. Today it has a much wider curriculum and is probably best known as the college of the late Professor Stephen Hawking. Bilney was an able student and made rapid progress in both branches of law—canon and civil. Due to his size, he was quickly nicknamed 'little Bilney' and the name stuck. He had a delicate constitution and

Figure 4: The original church at East Bilney

nervous disposition. Having such a shy and retiring nature would have made him difficult to know and Bilney probably passed most of his early student days alone. He lived in the shadow of others and was easily influenced, which may account to some degree for his wavering at his first trial.

Student life

Bilney's life as a student would have been very challenging and very different to student life today. There was the constant struggle to obtain books and keep well fed. Students would often be housed in inadequate rooms, lacking basic comforts and heating. The dropout rate for students was very high—some were not even too concerned to complete the course. Often students would be forced to beg and the goodwill between town and gown was often strained. Cambridge, in particular had a long history of animosity between town and university that would regularly flare up with misunderstanding and suspicion on both sides. As the new century dawned so, the university gained in power and influence, much to the chagrin of locals.

The process of study would be very different from modern times. Most of a student's time was spent not in the standard lectures, seminars and tutorials, but in solitude in rote learning (learning or memorisation by repetition), as books were scarce. Individual masters had more autonomy than their modern counterparts but had no guaranteed employment and were also in competition with one another. Students were more able to choose who their master would be, according to his status and popularity.

So, the life of the master, like student, could be unpredictable and precarious. Debates were popular but could be time consuming and sometimes of little value. Lectures, when they took place, were often long and tedious and would vary considerably in quality.[4] In general, university life was much less regulated than today.

At some point during his studies, Bilney transferred to focus fully on canon law studies and, according to the rules of the constitution, this would also have involved preparation for the priesthood. Whether this was the initial intention of Bilney, even before he commenced his studies, is not clear. He was certainly a very serious-minded man with a devotion to the Church. He would no doubt have made this decision in consultation with the master of the college. This would also have led him into continued residence at the college as a fellow to pursue studies further and perform priestly duties.[5]

Ordination

The year, 1519, was to be one of the most significant years in Bilney's life. It was the year when, amid the pomp of the Priory Church of St Bartholomew-the-Great at Smithfield, Bilney was ordained to the priesthood by the Bishop of Ely, Nicholas West. A year later he completed his Bachelor of Law, becoming a Fellow of Trinity Hall.[6] More important than ordination that year, was Bilney's coming to faith. Bilney led an austere life, rarely sleeping above four hours at night. He could not abide bad language and even found flippant singing an irritation, often protesting to his pupils about the 'dainty singing' of the clerks at church as a profane mockery to God. His disposition was such that even the sound of a flute drifting up the stairs from his neighbour, Thomas Thirlby, drove him to his knees in prayer![7]

It was not that Bilney was deliberately awkward and unsociable but rather was being awakened to his eternal needs. God was already graciously at work in his soul. As an ordained man, he had the outward appearance of religion—hard-working, dutiful and highly moral. He was as religiously informed as any of his day but, like Luther, he was preoccupied with thoughts of eternity and being right with God. At this stage it is difficult to be certain how much Bilney knew of the stirrings of discontent about the Church. From his upbringing and Norwich background, he may well have been influenced by Lollard teachings. Lollardy is the general term given to a movement originating in John Wycliff's teachings in the mid- 14th Century. The name *Lollard* was a derogatory nickname[8] but, by Bilney's time, it was regarded as heresy. Essentially it was a prototype of future Protestantism, striving against many of the teachings of the established Church and, along with Lutheranism, served as a seed bed for future Reformers. Norfolk had a long tradition of Lollardy and it may be that Bilney had some acquaintance with Lollard teachers. He certainly would have known of some of its basic teachings. There is some debate whether Bilney may have actually been a Lollard, or at least a secret one, but his intense devotion and loyalty to the Church makes this unlikely.[9]

The desperate search

During his time at Cambridge, Bilney became increasingly aware of the teachings of Martin Luther filtering into England. At first it seems the conscientious student avoided such influences, being preoccupied with his own studies and an ever-growing longing for peace within his own soul and assurance that he was accepted by God. This desire for assurance drove Bilney into an extreme lifestyle of asceticism. Like Luther, he sought every means possible, that the Church provided, to obtain this peace. He would endure long night vigils, often taking penances, and would attend every service possible, especially the Masses. He looked to the Church as a child to his father, not realizing that there would be no satisfaction, and being constantly reproached by his tender conscience. He so wanted peace with God and was at times tempted to seek solace outside the arms of the Church with the strange new teachings, but always pulled back for fear of offending the same God by any disobedience to the Church. Much later, in a letter to

Bishop Tunstall—who conducted Bilney's trial—he expressed his turmoil and frustration with the supposed pastor of his soul, in the following way,

> These are those physicians upon whom that woman that was twelve years vexed with the bloody flux had consumed all that she had, and felt no help, but was still worse and worse, until such time as she came at last unto Christ; and after she had once touched the hem of his vesture, through faith she was so healed, that by and by she felt the same in her body.[10]

It was the touch of the hem of Christ that Bilney longed for and continued in this wretched condition for many months. His efforts to find peace were frustrating and having a significant impact on his already weak constitution, not to mention his meagre financial resources. What Bilney, like so many, had not grasped was that salvation and peace with God could only come through One Mediator. It was grace, not works, through the medium of faith, and the future trumpet call of the Reformation that would meet this fundamental need.

It is perhaps hard for us to grasp how difficult it was for Thomas Bilney, a man of the Church. For centuries the gospel had been buried under so much rubble of church laws, superstition and plain ignorance, so little was available to help a searching man.

It was while wrestling in this state of despair that Bilney heard talk of a new book. The whispers among the cloisters of Cambridge spoke of such a book—a notorious book from the continent by a scholar called Erasmus. Bilney set out to get this book by all means. It was this book that would change his life for ever.

Notes

1 Beetleypc.norfolkparishes.gov.uk/a-short-history-of-old-beetley-beetley-and-east-bilney...

2 www.exploringnorfolkchurches.org/church/st-marys-east-bilney

3 Further information on the history and constitution of Trinity Hall can be found in: Roach, J.P.C. (Editor), *A History of the County of Cambridge and the Ise of Ely: vol 3, the City and University of Cambridge*, (London: Victoria County History, 1959), pp. 362–371. Also available online under British History Online. https://www.british-history.ac.uk/vch/cambs/vol3

4 Cobban, Alan, 'English University life in the Middle Ages' (Columbus: Ohio, 1999). Although predating our study, it gives a helpful indication of later student life. https://mtprof.msun.edu/Spr2000/MorgRev.html

5 Roach, J.P.C. (Editor), *A History of the County of Cambridge and the Ise of Ely: vol 3, the City and University of Cambridge*, pp. 362–371

6 https://en.wikipedia.org/wiki/Thomas_Bilney

7 Foxe, John, *The Acts and Monuments of John Foxe, a new and complete edition, Vol IV*: Stephen Cattley [Ed], (London: R.B. Seeley and W. Burnside, 1837), p. 621

8 Definition of Lollardy. It is most probably derived from the Dutch word, *lollen*—'to mutter'—and would have been used of Wycliff and his followers as a derogatory term. Another possible origin could be from the Latin, *lolium*, a possible reference to the Biblical parable of the tares, again implying something dangerous and heretical. A third possibility would be its derivation from the Franciscan named Lolhard, who converted to the Waldensians, regarded by the official church as a heretical group.

9 Maas, Korey, 'Thomas Bilney: "simple good soul"?' http://www.tyndale.org/tsj27/maas.html

10 Foxe, John, *The Acts and Monuments of John Foxe, a new and complete edition, Vol IV*, p. 635

2 The forbidden book

Oh, how I love your law! I meditate on it all day long. Your commands make me wiser than my enemies for they are ever with me (Psalm 119:97–98).

The seeds of the Reformation

It might seem strange to us that there could ever have been a time when the New Testament was considered dangerous, yet such a time existed.

As the 16th century opened, Europe entered into greater religious and political turmoil. The seeds of change had already been sown back in the 14th century. During the 15th century, a new outlook, popularly known as the Renaissance, was dominating European thinking. In a sense this is a complex idea involving a huge cultural and philosophical change in thinking—not easy to pinpoint in a few sentences. It did, however, prepare the mindset of Europe for great changes. In a sense the Renaissance was the bridge between the medieval and the modern world.

A narrower aspect of the Renaissance was the humanist movement which focused more on the literary—a looking back to the great Classical Age of the past. This created a restlessness in the minds of many, where the medieval outlook had been like a straitjacket on those longing for change. It became an increasingly popular movement among academics in the flourishing universities who were dissatisfied with the established church, its privileges and position. Scientific advance and exploration to new worlds were also beginning to open up minds. The medieval world was slowly making way for an exciting new age. A wind of change was blowing over Europe which was eventually to reach the shores of England.

In 1517, a German monk, by the name of Martin Luther, was to change the course of religious history in Europe for ever. Reared in the cradle of the Church, Luther began as a faithful and loyal son. Outwardly he was successful, climbing the ecclesiastical ladder, but inwardly he was in mental and spiritual conflict. Ever striving to

gain peace through an endless succession of good works, Luther despaired of ever finding such peace.

He finally found the sought-after peace, but not through his own works, but rather in the Biblical teaching of *justification by faith*. Reading the great letter of Romans, Luther wrestled with the meaning of the *righteousness of God*

Figure 5: Martin Luther described by Paul. Believing at first it was describing God's unapproachable holiness, he despaired. Then, while pouring over Paul's letter, the light finally dawned on Luther as he suddenly realized the true meaning. Paul was describing a righteousness that could be received by faith. Luther at last found peace, not in trying to earn his own righteousness but by receiving it through faith in Christ's finished work on the cross. Luther's life now took a different course. Under the hand of God, he was destined to pioneer a new work, or rather return to an old one—the everlasting and glorious gospel of God.

So it was that the nails were hammered, one morning, into the door of Wittenberg Church. A notice with 95 *theses* or points of debate threw down the challenge. This was initially in response to what Luther saw as the pernicious and unscriptural practice of selling indulgences—an ingenious system invented by the Papacy to pay for their pompous and outrageous lifestyle. Put simply, the believer, by payment of an indulgence (effectively a certificate), could help move their departed, loved one further along the path in Purgatory towards the happy release in Heaven.

Luther started a storm and eventually became a wanted man. As German princes and scholars gathered protectively around him, so Papal authorities determined to catch him and destroy him. Luther, knowing his course was set, began to write vigorously against the Catholic Church. The Reformation in Europe had begun.

As Luther wrote, aided by the recently invented Gutenberg printing press, so the writing reached English shores. News of his teaching quickly entered into the European universities. Luther's stand in Germany, in 1517, had thrown the religious world of Europe into uproar. The once almost invincible grip that the Roman Catholic Church had on the mind of the people was now broken. A new movement, variously termed Lutheranism or Protestantism was gaining momentum in Europe. It was not long before Luther's teachings filtered into England.

In 1509, Prince Henry Tudor came to the throne with the title Henry VIII. Tempestuous and vain-glorious, Henry had plunged into his kingship with vigour. Inheriting a good fortune from

Figure 6: Henry VIII

his father, he soon drained the coffers with ongoing wars and extravagant self-indulgence. Yet the one thing that eluded him was a future heir to the throne. Trapped in an unproductive marriage and an increasingly unhappy one to Catherine, the Spanish princess, his only solution seemed to be in ending it. For much of his time as English sovereign, Henry was locked in battle with the Papacy over his right to divorce and remarry.

This became Henry's driving obsession, leading eventually to the severing of England from the religious dominance of Rome. Unlike the Reformation movement on the continent, separation was, for Henry, for his own personal reasons. He was, to his dying day, a son of the Catholic Church, but was also a headstrong, pragmatic man. He was not renouncing his faith in the Roman Catholic Church, only his faith in Papal authority over his marriage. Henry was determined to have his way and used his position and power to drive the ecclesiastical machinery towards confrontation with Rome. At a deeper level, God was at work preparing the ground for a great change. It was the power of his very own Word that would break the bonds leading to the Reformation.

While, in Europe, it was Martin Luther who became the spark that fired the Reformation, in England there was no one personality. The Word of God was unleashed in two mighty Sources: Tyndale's *Translation* and Erasmus' *New Testament*.

Tyndale's part

No one can deny the significant role Tyndale played in the English Reformation. As a student of Oxford, Tyndale, like Bilney, discovered the liberating works of Humanism, which in turn led to the study of the New Testament. Tyndale was a most gifted linguist and continued his studies at Cambridge. It was probably at this

time—though it cannot be proved—that he may well have met Bilney and Latimer and even to have frequented the famous 'White Horse Inn' (See Chapter 3 to see why this Inn was famous). Tyndale became private chaplain and tutor to the children of Sir John Walsh and it was during his stay as chaplain that Tyndale formed his desire to produce a Bible in the English

Figure 7: William Tyndale

language. Tyndale found himself increasingly at odds with the local clergy and it was during one of these altercations that he uttered his most famous saying:

> I defy the Pope and all his laws; if God spare my life, ere many years, I will cause a boy that driveth the plough shall know more of the Scripture than thou dost.

Tyndale inevitably had to leave England for his own safety. He became a fugitive on the continent for the remainder of his life, but gave us his greatest legacy: his translation of the Bible.[1]

Desiderius Erasmus, the Dutch scholar, would have been known to Bilney through his works circulating around the university. Erasmus, a man of unusual ability, dedication and zeal, became one of the leading figures in the Humanist movement (not to be confused with modern day humanism) on the continent. Many Humanists were seizing on the opportunity to study the Scriptures afresh with the greater accessibility of Greek manuscripts. For most of them, it was a literary rather than spiritual curiosity that drove them to these studies. While Humanism of the day should not be equated with Protestantism, it was in many ways the significant forerunner. Many of the leading European Reformers began their search via the Humanist movement. These Humanists, while tolerated by the papal authorities, were viewed increasingly with suspicion as time went on.

Erasmus had visited England in 1499. His time was fruitful, making friends with many English scholars, though he was not impressed with the weather and the English beer! He even, for a time, became Professor at Queens College between 1510 –1515. Though, in 1499, he was a brilliant Latin scholar, Erasmus had at

that point no knowledge of Greek. It was a man by the name of John Colet, who introduced Erasmus to the ancient language, that inspired Erasmus to learn Greek. Returning to Europe, Erasmus devoted himself to the study of the language, eventually mastering it—such was his linguistic acumen. He then became very much a leading figure in the Humanist movement. While the author of many literary works, his

Figure 8: Dutch Scholar, Desiderius Erasmus

greatest achievement was his New Testament in Latin & Greek, the *Novum Instrumentum* (See Figure 9).

The first edition was published in 1516. It was dedicated to Pope Leo X, yet ironically it became the undoing of future papacy. In different editions it was used by both Tyndale and Luther in preparing their own translations of the Bible! It cannot be said that Erasmus was a Reformer in the strictest sense. Rather he very much remained a defender of the Church. He did, however, provide the key to open the Reformation. Or to change the analogy, the oft quoted saying, 'Erasmus laid the egg that Luther hatched.'[2]

Thus, through two independent sources—one from the renowned colleges of Oxford and the other

Figure 9: Page from the Novum Instrumentum

from the ancient halls of Cambridge—the work of reformation was built. It is the Cambridge story that chiefly concerns us and the significant part Bilney played in it.

Hidden treasure

It was a copy of this notorious book that now lay on the knees of Bilney. That night, light had come flooding through his soul, the cold and fear forgotten as he bathed in its glorious truths. Thereafter, each morning the book would be carefully hidden away like treasure while Bilney went about his scholastic duties. It must have been hard for the timid scholar as he thought about the hidden book. Would it be discovered? The thought set his heart pounding. How long before he could lay his hands once more on its precious contents?

Bilney, in a letter written later to Bishop Tunstall describes his reading:

> But at the last I heard speak of Jesus, even then when the New Testament was first set forth by Erasmus; which understanding to be eloquently done by him, and being allured rather by the Latin than for the word of God, (for at that time I knew not what it meant,) I bought it even by the providence of God, as I do now well understand and perceive: and at the first reading (as I well remember) I chanced upon this sentence of St. Paul, (O most sweet and comfortable sentence to my soul!) in 1 Tim. i. 15, 'It is a true saying, and worthy of all men to be embraced, that Christ Jesus came into the world to save sinners; of whom I am the chief and principal.' This one sentence, through God's instruction and inward working, which I did not then perceive, did so exhilarate my heart, being before wounded with the guilt of my sins, and being almost in despair, that immediately I felt a marvellous comfort and quietness, insomuch that my bruised bones leaped for joy.[3]

Like Luther discovering the true meaning of righteousness in Romans, so Bilney reasoned that if the very apostle Paul was the chief of sinners, then there was hope for him.

> Paul the chief of sinners! And yet Christ came to save him! Then why not me?

He had found, said Foxe:

> ... a better teacher than the doctors of canon law - the Holy Spirit of Christ.

At last, Bilney understood. He was acquitted not by his own works but by the grace of God through justification. He was a new man, a new creation in Christ. He now eagerly devoured the Scriptures and had a new desire for service to his fellow man:

> After this, the Scripture began to be more pleasant unto me than the honey or the honeycomb; wherein I learned, that all my travails, all my fasting and watching, all the redemption of masses and pardons, being done without trust in Christ, who only saveth his people from their sins; these, I say, I learned to be nothing else but even (as St. Augustine saith) a hasty and swift running out of the right way; or else much like to the vesture made of fig leaves, wherewithal Adam and Eve went about in vain to cover themselves, and could never before obtain quietness and rest, until they believed in the promise of God, that Christ, the seed of the woman, should tread upon the serpent's head: neither could I be relieved or eased of the sharp stings and bitings of my sins, before I was taught of God that lesson which Christ speaketh of in John iii.: Even as Moses exalted the serpent in the desert, so shall the Son of man be exalted, that all which believe on him should not perish, but have life everlasting.[4]

Bilney could not stop reading this treasure. Every moment possible was spent in study and prayer. Once safely locked away in his chambers, he hunched over the book, flickering candle in hand, pouring over the text. Pausing and lifting his eyes to heaven he would pray, asking for Divine help. With no human help available, the Holy Spirit alone was his teacher. Again, in a letter to Tunstall, he explained:

> At last I desired nothing more than that I, being so comforted by Him, might be strengthened by His Holy Spirit and grace from above, that I might teach the wicked His ways which are mercy and truth; and that the wicked might be converted unto Him by me who sometime also was wicked.[5]

Bilney was learning fast but not yet fully released from the Churches hold. As Marcus Loane comments:

> Bilney did not break away from the Church, even though he saw her sins with clear eyed reality; nor did he grasp the full stretch of reformation theology, even though he felt its power with increased understanding. But he was the first of the Cambridge scholars whose name is known to us to take his stand for the Reformation, and he was the central figure in a new school of evangelical life and witness in the University.[6]

This was the first victory for the New Testament in England but its reading was to have far greater implications for the gospel in England.

Notes

1 For a heart-warming account see: Edwards, Brian H., *God's Outlaw*, (Welwyn Garden City: Evangelical Press, 1976). Also, more recently: Lawson, Steven J., *The Daring Mission of William Tyndale*, (Sanford, Florida: Reformation Trust Publishing, 2014).

2 It is believed that this phrase originally came from an unknown monk in reference to Erasmus's seeming closeness to Luther in the Reformation cause which both denied. https://www.fromthebook.org/erasmus-laid-the-egg-that-luther-hatched/

3. Foxe, John, *The Acts and Monuments of John Foxe, a new and complete edition, Vol IV*, p. 635

4 Foxe, John, p. 635

5 Ibid, p. 635

6 Loane, Marcus, *Masters of the English Reformation*, (Church Book Room Press, 1954), p. 8

3 Cambridge evangelist

We are therefore Christ's ambassadors, as though God were
making his appeal through us. We implore you on Christ's behalf:
Be reconciled to God (2 Corinthians 5:20).

New creature in Christ

As Bilney grew in his understanding of his new-found faith so he looked out and around at his friends and colleagues. He was determined to share his great discovery with others. This would have taken immense courage for anyone in such times, let alone a man so shy and fearful. This is the mark of grace in the man and the Holy Spirit's boldness that he was given. His natural reserve was overcome by his desire to share the Good News. Bilney had no one to show him the way or train him; he was on his own. So, it was, this quiet scholar, more at home with his books, took the big step into personal evangelism. He became Christ's ambassador to Cambridge. What Bilney lacked, God more than made up for and personal evangelism was to prove his special gift. We could all learn much from this gracious evangelist. There is not a lot of detail regarding this period of Bilney's life, but what can be gleaned is most extraordinary. We do not know the full number of men Bilney influenced but among the more prominent are the following:

George Stafford

Stafford, was an established classics scholar, well known for his lectures. He had a popular style and students flocked to hear him. Like Bilney, Stafford was searching and found in Bilney the one who could unlock the Scriptures. He was led to faith by Bilney and his lectures were radically transformed. A younger student at that time, Thomas Brecon, later to have significant influence in the courts of Edward VI and Elizabeth, reflected on Stafford's prowess. When speaking of him, he once said:

> When master Stafford read and master Latimer preached then was Cambridge blessed.[1]

Very significantly, both these men attributed their conversions, humanly speaking to the little evangelist, Bilney.

Around 1528, Stafford visited a colleague, who had gone down with the plague, that was then ravaging the countryside. His sick friend was known to be something of a conjuror in the University. (The expression, 'conjuror', may have had a more sinister meaning than it has today.) Stafford made it his business not only to bring comfort to his friend but to point him to Christ. He achieved his goal—the man trusting Christ and even burning his books—but Stafford himself caught the plague and died as a consequence. He bequeathed his books to the University.[2]

Thixtill Dixit!

John Thixtill, perhaps the least known in this group, was a fellow of Pembroke Hall and a close colleague of George Stafford. While little is known of Thixtill, his fame as a scholar must have been considerable, and can be judged by his nickname, 'Thixtill Dixit'— an honourable nickname really, since this was a play on the Latin phrase, *'Ipse Dixit'*, meaning literally, 'he himself said it'. It would seem this was a reference to Thixtill's confident assertiveness.[3] He was quite clearly a man of some standing and confidence. We do not know in what way Bilney impacted his life, but we see him along with his close friend, Stafford, in the company of Bilney, listening to his exposition of Scripture and the way of Life. He was also a regular attendee of the famous White Horse Inn.

John Lambert: Evangelical fugitive

John Lambert, born Nicholson, also of Norfolk, likewise found his way into Bilney's circle. Educated at Queens College, he later became a close friend of Thomas Cromwell, one of Henry's key architects in the Reformation. While at Cambridge he came to faith through Bilney's influence and also joined the White Horse group. Owing to his outspoken views, it soon became necessary for him to leave England and seek refuge in Antwerp. He changed his name from Nicholson for safety and gained the position of a priest to an English factory. While on the continent, he rubbed shoulders with other exiles such as John Frith and William Tyndale. Returning in 1531, the year of Bilney's death, he continued his teaching but was carefully watched. In 1536, he was accused of heresy for denying the teaching of transubstantiation and the real presence of Christ in the bread. Managing to escape, he led a precarious life as a fugitive before being once more captured and eventually burnt at the stake in 1536.[4] It is said that while burning, Thomas Cromwell, his one-time colleague but now opponent, watched from a window with tears in his eyes. As the flames leapt Lambert cried,

None but Christ, none but Christ![5]

Matthew Parker

Perhaps most notable of all was a later Archbishop of Canterbury,

Matthew Parker. Also, a son of Norfolk, Parker went to Corpus Christi, Cambridge and made great progress. Wolsey had his eye on the young scholar as a potential leader for his own new college at

Oxford, but Parker, like Thomas Cranmer, declined. Instead, he too came under the influence of Bilney and the Cambridge group. He continued to rise in authority, especially under Anne Boleyn's patronage. Parker's success continued during Edward's brief reign, becoming a close friend of Martin Bucer, the European Reformer, but when Mary came to the throne his life became more precarious. On the succession of Elizabeth, Parker was

Figure 10: A Future Archbishop, Matthew Parker

appointed Archbishop in 1559. Perhaps, unfairly, owing to his intense inquisitiveness as archbishop, he may be the reason for the phrase 'Nosey Parker'![6]

His influence on preaching

Thomas Arthur was to become one of Bilney's closest friends. Also a Norfolk man, he probably entered Trinity Hall and was converted to Protestant views by Bilney, or at least certainly influenced. He became a fellow of St Johns (1517–18) as Master of Arts and in 1518, principal of St Mary's Hostel. This is probably the place identified as the leper hospital.[7] He later embarked on a preaching tour with Bilney. More will be said of this later.

Another outstanding preacher was Robert Barnes, who became a high-profile Reformer. He also first came into contact with the gospel via Bilney at Cambridge and was also among the White Horse group. He graduated as Doctor of Divinity in 1523 and, soon after, was made Prior of his Cambridge Convent. Bilney saw the potential in Barnes and encouraged him in his preaching. On Christmas Eve, Barnes preached a fiery sermon at St Edwards Church, Cambridge, against the clerical pomp and religious abuse of the day. This resulted in a storm, leading to charges of heresy. In 1526, Barnes was summoned before the ecclesiastical authorities and forced to recant.

Although recanting, Barnes still supported the cause. Even in prison he was involved in smuggling contraband copies of the Bible. Escaping, he made his way to the Continent, meeting with other Reformers, including Martin Luther. Barnes was able to return to England in 1531, acting as an intermediary between the English government and the Lutherans, in the hope of securing their support for Henry's divorce. He fell out of favour when Henry hardened his views against Lutheranism and Barnes preached a sermon against Bishop Gardiner—a future scourge of Protestantism. In July of 1540, as Anne of Cleves was divorced by Henry, Barnes suffered martyrdom at the stake.[8]

Although an impressive list and a remarkable testimony to the dedication of Bilney, the biggest prize was yet to be, and that was the rising star of Hugh Latimer.

Bilney's secret!

Thus, Bilney's early influence on the future Reformation in England can hardly be understated. He seems to have managed to engage with so many leading figures, and there is no knowing how many other students and colleagues he had influenced. What was the secret of his extraordinary success? We may never fully know but we can guess.

Firstly, Bilney, once he had caught hold of the glorious truths of Salvation, never seemed to lose his zeal and had a genuine love and concern for the lost. He never seemed to have got over the fact that Christ died for such a sinner. As already quoted in a letter to Tunstall, it was his desire to reach out to the lost. In Bilney, we see the words of Peter fulfilled:

> But in your hearts revere Christ as Lord. Always be prepared to give an answer to everyone who asks you to give the reason for the hope that you have. But do this with gentleness and respect (1 Peter 3:15).

Again, in Colossians 4:6:

> Let your conversation be always full of grace, seasoned with salt, so that you may know how to answer everyone.

Perhaps knowing his own limitations and fear of the limelight, he made it his business to work quietly in personal evangelism. His gentle character certainly made him approachable and his warm spirit easy to confide in. Whatever else, Bilney stands before us as a great example in personal evangelism.

Of his learning we know little, though Latimer gives us a hint when he said:

> As for his singular learning, as well in Holy scripture as in all other good letters, I will not speak of it.[9]

As to his literary remains, there is little since none of his sermon notes remain and nothing else to our knowledge was written by him. There are some letters written to Bishop Tunstall in Latin, translated by Foxe—already quoted—that shall be referred to again. Also, some annotated notes left in Bilney's *Vulgate Bible*! We are indebted to J E Batley for bringing these to public notice with the publication of a book on Bilney and his Bible in 1940.[10] After his death, Bilney's friends treasured his copy of the *Vulgate* with notes in the margins. It is now in the Corpus Christi College Library. The date, 1520, is written in it suggesting this was the date it was acquired.

These notes give a precious insight into Bilney's developing understanding of the Bible. They show his working through the Bible from Genesis to Malachi. At this point the notes come to an end, suggesting that he may have switched to the New Testament using his *Novum Testamentum* or else it could have stopped due to his trial and imprisonment in 1527.[11]

The White Horse gatherings

Reference has been made to the White Horse Inn (See Figure 5). This was to become the epicentre of the reforming work in Cambridge. It was with growing alarm that the ecclesiastical authorities saw Cambridge now as a hotbed of the subversive teachings of Luther. Between the years of 1525 and 1526, there is clear evidence of meetings taking place at the White Horse Inn, but it is likely that they were taking place before this date. Much has been said about these famous meetings, so much so that they have slipped into

Figure 11: Plaque at the site of The White Horse Inn

Reformation folk law and some extravagant claims have been made that they formed the basis of the English Reformation movement! They certainly were a place for meeting, where new ideas could be swapped and shared. Without doubt, Luther's teachings would have been discussed, so much so that it earned the nickname, 'Little Germany'. The obvious connection being with Luther, and not, as one scholar suggested, the reference to German Beer! (Beer being still a relatively new habit to imbibe in public Houses).[12]

At the hub of this group was Bilney, later joined by Latimer, Ridley, Coverdale, Cranmer, Barnes and many others—possibly as many as thirty leading figures at one time or another. It almost reads like a 'Who's who of the English Reformation.' It is possible that Tyndale would also have been among the number during his stay at Cambridge. Out of this group, two would become archbishops, seven would become bishops and eight would be martyred for their faith.[13]

Steven Lawson has reflected that:

> These informal gatherings became the kindling for the English Reformation that would soon spread like wildfire across the British Isles.[14]

The Inn was originally located on the site of King's Lane to the west of Kings Parade. When the Kings College Screen was extended in 1870, the tavern was demolished but a plaque on the Colleges Chetwynd Court commemorates this (See Fig. 11).

Caring for the outcasts

It was not just the personal salvation of a soul that motivated Bilney but, like his Saviour, he was compassionate for the whole man. Again, like his master, 'he went around doing good' (Acts 10:38). We can only marvel at his capacity for hard work. Alongside his university duties, discussions and devotions, he managed to fit in a regular round of prison visits, seeking by whatever means to relieve their suffering and share his faith. He was often seen about the city succoring the needs of the poor and desolate, often providing sustenance out of his own resources, and spending time among the sick, especially the 'lazar cots'—houses for the reception of the sick and leprous.[15] This may well have been the same hospital, mentioned earlier, that Thomas Arthur was involved with and may also account for their close friendship. The hospital had its origins dating back to the Crusades and is one of the oldest buildings in the area. At the hospital, Bilney would mix freely with the inmates at great personal risk, even bandaging their wounds and offering words of hope and comfort. When one remembers that this was the 16th century and imagines what must have been the relatively primitive nature of medical care and sanitary conditions, it was a task of bravery and mercy. Bilney maintained this humble ministry for several years and even induced Latimer, when converted, to join him.

Yet, with all this busyness, Bilney made time for prayer.

We can see him very early, before the dawn breaks, on his knees in his cold chamber, hands clasped, and eyes raised. It is all quiet as the university sleeps. A pale shaft of light pierces the room and the tower bells usher in a new day, but still the small figure does not stir. Lost in prayer, he is laying the whole university community before his Lord in supplication: perhaps individuals he has noticed struggling; the steely opposition of clerics; a lost soul of a prisoner; prayers for protection;

> *and guidance for the day ahead. He opens his eyes and slowly rises, shaking off the cold and cramp. Aware that the forces of darkness are slowly surrounding him and time is running out, the spectre of martyrdom already beckoning him, he prepares for a new day.*

Such was the character of this remarkable man that history seems to have conspired to forget.

Notes

1 *Writings of the Rev Thomas Breckon*, (Presbyterian Board of Publication, 1843), p. 7

2 *Writings of the Rev Thomas Breckon*, p. 7

3 Attwater, Aubrey, *A Short History of Pembroke College Cambridge*, (Cambridge: Pembroke College, 1973), p. 31

4 https://en.wikipedia.org/wiki/John_Lambert_(martyr)

5 Ibid

6 https://en.wikipedia.org/wiki/Matthew_Parker

7 https://www.cambridgeppf.org/pages/category/cambridge-leper-chapel

8 https://en.wikipedia.org/wiki/Robert_Barnes_(martyr)

9 Latimer, Hugh, *Sermons and Remains of Hugh Latimer*, (Cambridge: The University Press, 1845), p. 330

10 Batley, J.Y., *On a Reformer's Latin Bible, being an essay on the adversaria in the vulgate of Thomas Bilney*, (Cambridge: Deighton Bell & Co, 1940).

11 Loane, Marcus, *Masters of the English Reformation*, pp. 29–30

12 https://whitehorseinn.org/resource-library/articles/why-we-call-our-radio-program-white-horse-inn/

13 Lawson, Stephen, J., *The Daring Mission of William Tyndale*, p. 7

14 Ibid, p. 7

15. Foxe, John, *Vol IV*, p. 620

4 Latimer's conversion

But whatever were gains to me I now consider loss for the sake of Christ. What is more, I consider everything a loss because of the surpassing worth of knowing Christ Jesus my Lord, for whose sake I have lost all things (Philippians 3:7–8).

Early years

While Bilney was busy at Trinity Hall, Hugh Latimer—the sturdy opponent of reform—was preparing himself for future service in the Church. God would indeed use this able man but first he had to meet with Bilney and have his life changed.

Latimer was probably born in 1485 but there is some uncertainty about the date. He came from farming family in Thurcaston, Leicestershire. Latimer entered Clare College, Cambridge, where he studiously set himself to work. Being a faithful son of the Church and noted for his ability, he made rapid progress, completing his Masters (MA) in April 1514 and ordination as a priest in July of the following year. Bilney, at this point, had noticed Latimer's academic stature and his devotion to the Church. He was very much in awe of Latimer, and this would increase when, in 1522, Latimer was nominated to the position of university preacher and chaplain. This was a prestigious position for so young a man. While carrying out his official duties, he continued with theological studies and received the Bachelor of Divinity degree in 1524. Latimer was aware of the rumblings of dissent among certain Cambridge scholars, and did his utmost to warn young students and turn them away from the pernicious teachings of Bilney and his friends. Yet, God had his hand on Latimer and was going to bring him into confrontation with Bilney, but in a most wonderful way. Latimer stood like a Goliath, highly gifted, well positioned with the full backing of an army of ecclesiastical and secular authorities behind him. Bilney, on the other hand, resembled young David, small by comparison and seemingly modestly equipped. Yet the battle was the Lord's and God was clearly on Bilney's side. The confrontation did not take place on the field of battle or even in the halls of debate but in the quiet chambers of Latimer's room, in the form of a simple 'confession'.

Latimer's lecture

In the spring of 1524, there was a great bustle of activity as students packed into the Great St Mary's Church in Cambridge. Some, unable to get a seat, were content to remain standing at the back—among them was Thomas Bilney. Dignitaries of the Church and University were already seated in rows, displaying their ecclesiastical robes

Figure 12: Hugh Latimer

and finery. As a young man ascended the pulpit there was a quietening and a fixing of eyes on the pulpit figure. The lecturer looked out on the vast congregation. With hands leaning on either side of the pulpit, he glanced briefly at his notes and began. This was Hugh Latimer, about to give his disputation—a refutation of the ideas of the Reformer, Philip Melanchthon. The subject that would earn his divinity degree.

Melanchthon (1497–1560), was second in rank only to Luther. He was the perfect complement to Luther's fiery genius, steadying and systematizing Luther's ideas. An able theologian of note on the continent, his writings were a constant source of anger for the Church of Rome. He particularly incensed the authorities by his precise and well-argued teaching on the Lord's Supper, attacking the standard view of the Church. Latimer launched into his counterattack on Melanchthon. He spoke with such eloquence and ability, much to the delight of the majority present. The officials beamed. Here was a home-grown champion in the making—a man who might one day rid England of the Protestant curse.

> At the back, Bilney watched and listened with growing sadness as Latimer continued to blast Melanchthon's views. Bilney sighed, recognizing in Latimer his own former ways. He also longed that somehow, in some way, he might be able to influence this man for good. As the disputation ended and people left their seats, congregated and chatted, Bilney remained sitting, stunned by Latimer's eloquence, fists clenched in frustration. He heard the buzz of excitement in people's voices and slowly got up from his seat, head bowed. He kept thinking, 'This man is so able, but he does not know Christ as I do. If only I could point him to my blessed Saviour.' Bilney turned to leave, lost in thought. How could he win this man for Christ?

Marcus Loane, summed up Bilney's dilemma,

He was only Little Bilney, and would never do any great service for

God; but let him win the soul of that one man, and what great things would he do in His Name.[1]

> *Bilney, under God's hand, had been successful in pointing others to Christ, but this man was different. There was an air of arrogance, of confidence, that made Bilney nervous. The answer was to get an interview with Latimer. As Bilney passed through the jostling crowds back to his rooms, he thought about the way he could meet Latimer. He must somehow speak with this man. As he made his way slowly back through the crowded streets, so he lifted a silent prayer to God. Back in his study, he sat wearily down. Struggling to hold back the tears, Bilney bowed his head again in prayer.*

Bilney's 'confession'

Hugh Latimer was not unaware of the fermenting of Reformation ideas in the college and would have heard of the change in Bilney with some alarm. Being a priest and a zealot for the Catholic Church, he made it his duty to publicly attack and discredit the evangelical truths Bilney and others espoused. Like Saul of Tarsus, he pursued the newly converted men, pitting all his intellectual powers against the Truth. But in a meeting with Bilney, he was soon to experience a 'Damascus Road' conversion that would make him the 'Apostle of the Reformation' in England. Bilney perceived Latimer's potential and sought by all means to win him. Here was a man who, if once changed, could become a mighty preacher of the gospel. Knowing that the 'battle is the Lord's' (1 Samuel 17:47), he determined to challenge and defeat the intellectual Goliath of Cambridge with the 'sword of the Spirit' (Ephesians 6:17).

After much prayer, Bilney hit upon the perfect plan. He would share his testimony with Latimer as a confession. He would go before him as penitent to priest. He reckoned that Latimer would seize the opportunity to have Bilney, a penitent, return to the fold. Having resolved his course of action, Bilney again committed his plan to prayer.

Early the next morning Bilney set off for Latimer's quarters, his heart pounding at the thought of the risk he was taking. With heavy footsteps he climbed the stairs to Latimer's rooms. Passing few people at that early hour, he found himself at last at the door of Latimer's chambers. Great fear came over him as he paused before knocking. He could feel his perspiration trickling down his neck, his hands trembling. Perhaps this was not the right way? There were others more suitably qualified than him. Would the great Latimer even consider his confession? He could feel his resolve melting and quickly lifted his eyes to heaven. Just then, a young student came bounding past, so Bilney quickly rapped sharply on the door. After a pause he knocked again—there was no going back now. Eventually the door was pulled open, and Latimer stood in the frame. He was surprised to see Bilney standing there and coldly acknowledged him. Bilney bowed respectfully and asked permission to have his confession heard. Latimer paused, unsure how to react, then smiled thinly and widened the door, motioning with his hand for Bilney to enter. He had urgent business that morning, but it could wait. Here before him was the very ringleader of the troublesome group. Surely such a confession was a virtual admission of his errors. A son of the Church could be won back from error.

Inside, Latimer gathered his robes and sat down. Bilney stumbled to his knees before him and waited. With a nod of the head Latimer gave him leave to confess his sins. Prostrating himself before Latimer, with faltering words, Bilney shared honestly how God had saved him. He related how, in anguish of soul, he had sought salvation and had found the blood of Christ as his only hope. He spoke of his night with the open bible before him and the wonderful words of hope flooding into his soul He referred to himself as a chief sinner but cleansed by the blood of Christ. Latimer listened and his eyes widened as he heard the honest 'confession'. Bilney paused and looked up at the priest. His heart leapt within as he saw not anger but thoughtful concern on the face of Latimer.

For his own part Latimer was captivated by the transparent sincerity and earnestness of the confessor before him. As he continued to listen, the Holy Spirit powerfully applied Bilney's simple testimony like a two-edged sword, piercing Latimer's proud heart. Thoughts and feelings welled up as the 'confession' stirred his own heart with a longing for certainty. As the Truth gripped his mind and soul, so the priest became the penitent, while the supposed 'penitent' pointed to the Great High Priest. At the end of the 'confession' Latimer sat stunned—he had never heard such things before. Now his own heart was laid bare, and he was ready to seek this wonderful Saviour for himself.

Reflecting on this encounter Latimer said:

> Bilney, desired me for God's sake to hear his confession. I did so; and so, saw the truth by his confession I learned more than before in many years.[2]

Latimer transformed

Over the next few days, a revolution took place in Latimer. Trusting Christ alone, he abandoned the schoolmen for the Scriptures. He sought out the company of like-minded men and frequented the famous White Horse Inn, much to the consternation of former friends. He and Bilney were now almost inseparable. They would often spend time together in earnest conversation, roaming the outskirts of Cambridge. A favourite haunt was Castle Hill (see Figure 13), where they were seen so often that

Figure 13: Castle Hill, also known as Heretics Hill

it was nicknamed *Heretics Hill*. Latimer now became Bilney's constant companion, spending much time in prayer and study. Like a Barnabas, Bilney became the guide and encourager to his more illustrious friend.

Latimer's transformation also impacted his preaching with new light. He had obtained his own copy of the New Testament and was devouring it. His preaching was electrified as he preached Christ crucified and denounced many Papal abuses. Unlike Bilney and others, there was a quality in his preaching that was unmatched in power. Bilney must have looked on with intense joy as he saw his protégé developing. Here was no ordinary preacher but a man fit to meet the task—a true preacher of the Reformation. Latimer preached regularly in the pulpit of St Edward's Church. He also took opportunities to preach further afield. Towards the close of 1525, complaints were beginning to arrive at the Bishop of Ely's door about the fire-brand preacher. The Bishop decided to hear for himself what Latimer was saying. A surprise visit was made to Great St Mary's, where Latimer was once preaching. The service had hardly begun when the Bishop, with his retinue, entered. With quick thinking, Latimer changed his sermon and preached on the Priesthood of Christ. The Bishop responded favourably and asked Latimer to preach again, only this time against the doctrines of Luther. Latimer responded:

> My lord, I am not acquainted with the doctrine of Luther, nor are we permitted to read his works; and therefore, it was but a vain thing for me to refute his doctrine, not understanding what he hath written nor what opinion he holdeth.

Perhaps this was not the best response, as the Bishop sensed an evasion and retorted:

> Very well, Mr Latimer, I perceive that you somewhat smell of the pan; you will repent of this gear one day.[3]

From that day on, the Bishop of Ely sought to frustrate Latimer's opportunities within his diocese and had some measured success. This, however, was short lived when Cardinal Wolsey heard of it and sought an explanation from Latimer. On hearing the details of the sermon and that he had preached no other dangerous doctrine,

Wolsey, who admired Latimer's openness and style, overruled the Bishop:

> If the Bishop of Ely cannot abide such doctrine as you have here repeated, you shall have my license and preach it unto his beard, let him say what he will.[4]

So, Latimer was merely cautioned, but given license to preach in all parts of England. While taking every opportunity to extend his preaching, Latimer was continuing to learn from Bilney's example. He saw how Bilney prayed, witnessed and served. Latimer joined Bilney on his prison visits and helped care for the poor and sick.

On one occasion, they aided a poor woman who had been falsely accused of the murder of her child. They procured a Kings Pardon, setting her free.[5]

On another occasion, there was a wife of an officer who had been thrown into prison on the grounds of adultery. Such was the gracious impact of Bilney's care and witness, that she was led to Christ and repented of her sins. She was now ready to receive her punishment knowing Christ had died for her sins.[6]

All the while, through Bilney's example, God was preparing Latimer, the future apostle of the Reformation. Up to this point, Bilney and Latimer, though carefully watched, were unmolested, but things were soon to change.

This change took place on Christmas Eve, 1525, with the sermon of Robert Barnes, already referred to.[7] The furor following, meant Bilney and Latimer had to take greater care. Eventually, they were both summoned to appear before Wolsey and his court. Even so, Wolsey does not appear too harsh with them, especially Latimer, who seems to have been something of a favourite with Wolsey. Latimer retained his license with little impact. Bilney, though not suffering like Barnes, had his costs paid, but was forced to declare an oath concerning his future preaching. He had to promise to cease from preaching Lutheran heresy.

Sadly, Bilney complied with this stricture and for a time was compromised in his preaching and conscience. We may reproach him for this, but need to realize that Bilney, for all his achievements, was a man like us and prone to fail. It would happen again later on in his life with more serious implications.

Notes

1 Loane, Marcus, *Masters of the English Reformation*, p. 7
2 Latimer, Hugh, 'Sermon on the Lord's Prayer', *Sermons by Hugh Latimer, Sometime Bishop of Worcester, Martyr, 1555*, (Cambridge: The University Press, 1844), p. 334
3 Hannula, Richard, M., *Hugh Latimer, Bitesize Biographies*, (Welwyn Garden City: Evangelical Press, 2013), p. 25
4 Hannula, Richard, M., *Hugh Latimer, Bitesize Biographies*, p. 28
5 Latimer, Hugh, Sermons by *Hugh Latimer, Sometime Bishop of Worcester, Martyr, 1555*, pp. 335–336
6 Foxe, John, *Vol IV*, p. 621
7 Loane, Marcus, p. 15

5 Bilney preaching

How, then, can they call on the one they have not believed in? And how can they believe in the one of whom they have not heard? And how can they hear without someone preaching to them?
(Romans 10:14).

The Cardinal's College

One of Cardinal Wolsey's dreams for glory was to have a college in Oxford, created and named after him, Cardinal College. He had been on the lookout for able men to teach and had succeeded in finding several Cambridge men. These included a number of scholars influenced by Bilney, but Wolsey, though aware of this, was more concerned with ability than conviction and, in his blind desire to honour his own name, pursued his aims despite warnings from others. The upshot of this was the influence of Reformation teachings in the hallowed halls of Oxford. In 1527, a supply chain of Bibles and other 'seditious books' had been traced from the continent to a London base, for circulation in England. The key figure turned out to be Thomas Garret, a rector of the church of All Hallows, Honey Lane, Cheapside. A former graduate of Oxford, Garret had been supplying books to the University. But worse, the source went direct to the Cardinal's College! The capture of Garret inevitably led to a purge in Oxford. A search was made, and the incriminating evidence found. A whole group of about a dozen scholars was rounded up and imprisoned in an underground cellar beneath the college. The men were kept in appalling conditions, worsened by the fact that the cellar was used for storing salted fish. During their confinement three men died, and the rest suffered slowly in health owing to the damp, cold and unwholesome conditions. Only two finally survived the ordeal. One

of these, Betts, later became Anne Boleyn's chaplain. The other, John Frith, survived and continued, under great threat, to serve the cause before eventually dying a martyr's death in 1533 at Smithfield, London.

The Oxford purge, along with the events in Cambridge around Barnes' trial, put a check on the reformation work but did not stop its course.

Figure 14: Cardinal Wolsey

Opposition to reform would further increase as we shall see with Bilney's approaching trial. His course was being played out and he had done enough to start a work that could never be stopped. Also, other men, especially Latimer, were now taking centre stage.

Norfolk preaching tour

We do not know for certain what changed Bilney's mind, but in the spring of 1527, he decided to set out on a preaching tour. The restrictions placed upon the content of his preaching would have been agonizing. In addition, seeing his friend, Latimer, able to preach freely, would have further aggravated this censure. The run of university teaching could no longer satisfy him. He was so aware of the momentous times he was living in. This, combined with his sensitive conscience, would have made it increasingly intolerable for him to remain silent. Like Paul he would have cried out:

Woe! To me if I do not preach the gospel (1 Corinthians 9:16).

So, Bilney, in the company of his trusted friend Thomas Arthur, set out from Cambridge to his native Norfolk. There is not much detail of this tour except what is recorded by Foxe. From the records we have, it is clear that Bilney did not hold back in openly declaring the truths of a simple gospel. Bilney knew he was flying in the face of the promise he made to Wolsey but reasoned he had to obey Christ rather than men. Bilney still did not have a clear grasp of all aspects of salvation. There was still much of the loyal

Figure 15: Thomas Bilney plucked from the pulpit

Catholic in him, but he did have a firm hold on the efficacy of Christ and Christ alone to save men from sin, and that was what he preached.

We get some idea of the impact by the reaction he received on his travels. While the common people heard him gladly, no doubt finding his bold preaching a novelty, the religious establishment was enraged. Twice while he was at Ipswich, he was literally pulled out of the pulpit—such was the rage of his opponents (See Figure 15).

Undeterred, he continued his tour, eventually moving from the eastern counties, then south towards London. In the parish church of Willesden, he urged the people to forsake idolatry and trust only Christ. The Whitson week saw him at the church of St Magnus', where he spoke strongly against image worship and the intercession of saints. Finally, it was too much for the authorities, and under the instruction of the Bishop of London, the two preachers were thrown into the Bishop's own coal house, before being taken to the Tower of London on a charge of heresy.

We can gain something of the nature of Bilney's preaching from the following recollections of 'witnesses', called to support the claim of heresy—again faithfully recorded by Foxe. They vary in style, and range across a series of charges given by Bilney against the church. There were also tender appeals to turn to Christ for salvation.

Examples of Bilney's preaching

In Christ Church, Ipswich, he attacked the superstitions of the Church. Once, when speaking on the efficacy of Christ as the only Mediator, he cried out that the 'cowl of St Francis wrapped around a dead body had no power to take away sin.'

In another sermon at Ipswich he preached,

> Our Saviour Christ is our Mediator between us and the Father: what should we need then to seek any saint for remedy? Wherefore, it is great injury to the blood of Christ, to make such petitions, and blasphemeth our Saviour.

On another occasion:

> That man is so imperfect of himself, that he can in no wise merit by his own deeds.

Again:

> The coming of Christ was long prophesied before, and desired by the prophets: but John the Baptist, being more than a prophet, did not only prophesy, but with his finger showed him, saying, 'Behold the Lamb of God, which taketh away the sins of the world.' Then, if this were the very Lamb, which John did demonstrate, which taketh away the sins of the world, what injury is it to our Saviour Christ, that to be buried in St. Francis' cowl should remit four parts of penance! What is then left to our Saviour Christ, which taketh away the sins of the world? This I will justify to be a great blasphemy to the blood of Christ.

On the question of pilgrimages and miracles he had the following to say:

> It was a great folly to go on pilgrimage, and that preachers, in times past, have been antichrists; and now it hath pleased God somewhat to show forth their falsehood and errors. 'The people have used foolishly of late pilgrimages, which for them had been better they had been at home.'
>
> The miracles done at Walsingham, at Canterbury, and there, in Ipswich, were done by the devil, through the sufferance of God, to blind the poor people: and that the pope hath not the keys that Peter had, except he follows Peter in his living.

In the Parish of Willesden, Foxe comments that he,

> Exhorts the people to put away their gods of silver and gold and leave their offerings unto them; for that such things as they offered have been known oftentimes afterward to have been given to the vilest of women. Also, that Jews and Saracens would have become Christian men long ago, had it not been for the idolatry of Christian men, in offering of candles, wax, and money, to stocks and stones.

From his Whitson sermon at St Magnus, London:

> First, he said, 'Pray you only to God, and to no saints,' rehearsing the Litany; and when he came to 'Sancta Maria, ora pro nobis,' that is, 'Holy Mary pray for us,' he said, 'Stay there.'

Again:

> Christian men ought to worship God only, and no saints.

He then added:

> Christian people should set up no light before the images of saints: for saints in heaven need no light, and the images have no eyes to see.
>
> As Hezekiah destroyed the brazen serpent that Moses made by the commandment of God; even so should kings and princes now-a-days destroy and burn the images of saints set up in churches.

Such was Bilney's bold preaching. It is perhaps hard for us to fully grasp how daring such preaching was. When we also remember that he was still working through his own understanding of the gospel, it becomes all the more remarkable.

Against the papacy

Most daring of all, he preached vehemently against the Papacy:

> These five hundred years there hath been no good pope, and in all the times past, we can find but fifty: for they have neither preached, nor lived well, or conformably to their dignity; wherefore, till now, they have borne the keys of simony. Against them, good people! We must preach and teach unto you, for we cannot come to them; it is a great pity they have sore slandered the blood of Christ.

Some of his words were very hard hitting:

The preachers before this have been antichrists, and now it hath pleased our Saviour Christ to show their false errors, and to teach another way and manner of the holy gospel of Christ, to the comfort of your souls.

Then added:

I trust that there shall and will come other besides me, which shall show and preach to you the same faith and manner of living that I do show and preach to you, which is the very true gospel of our Saviour Christ, and the mind of the holy fathers, whereby you shall be brought from their errors, wherein you have been long seduced; for before this there have been many that have slandered you, and the gospel of our Saviour Christ.

The portrait of Bilney that emerges, is of a man energized and filled with the Spirit. This was not the old Bilney, retiring, shy and timid, but a man on a mission. He and his fellow preacher, Arthur, had blazed a trail across the counties. Moving from place to place in those days cannot have been easy. The physical weariness of travel, staying at taverns with an ever-increasing uncertainty of the kind of response his preaching might produce, would have taxed the bravest of men.

What kind of a preacher was he? What he lacked in presence, he must have made up for in content. He was not a natural preacher like Latimer, gifted with eloquence and presence, but he spoke with passion and earnestness. A preaching novelty, he must have drawn crowds, for he got the attention of local churchmen. His preaching was bold and direct, yet clearly intended for the masses, and therefore would have probably been couched in simple language.

He preached as his heart burned, principally of his own love of Christ, the Saviour and Mediator. There is no doubt that he would have included his own testimony as he sought to convey the life-changing power of the gospel. At times he got impassioned and probably spoke unwisely, but his heart yearned to see the ignorant and confused, enlightened.

How clear his beliefs in Protestant truths were, is hard to ascertain, but he extolled the central truths of faith alone in Christ. He was also unwavering in his attacks on many abuses of the Church, but these were still early days in Reformation thought and there must have still been many aspects yet to work out. We must, nevertheless, credit Bilney, however marred with the grace and zeal for his Master, to go out and preach in such difficult circumstances and in such perilous times.

In addition to his preaching, Bilney showed that he was an able debater. Long nights spent in prayer, with the New Testament at his knees, had taught him much. Perhaps, he was more at home in debate than in the pulpit. This was more familiar ground and he clearly showed his aptness and quick mind.

Bilney and Friar Brusierd

During his preaching travels, he would often be challenged by local, preaching friars. A protracted debate between a Friar Brusierd and Bilney was written up by Brusierd and later used as evidence against Bilney. If these are fair accounts, then it is hardly surprising that such preaching would charge Bilney, already a marked man, with heresy These were some of the many charges brought against Bilney and Arthur, and used by later witnesses at Bilney's trial. It is a long-protracted account given by Foxe, but the essence of which is as follows:

Friar Brusierd accused Bilney of blasphemy in his preaching, yet stressed that he comes to help Bilney, pitying his disposition, but insisting he errs on three grounds.

1. Preaching error with such vehemence taking advantage of ignorant people.
2. Pouring contempt on the precious blood of Christ.
3. Denying the efficacy of the intercession of Saints.

Bilney's response was incredulity that such unscriptural views of intercession persisted. Referring to them as 'babbling', alluding to the Sermon on the Mount, and quotes from Matthew 6:8 and 1 Timothy 2:5, adding:

> If then there be but one mediator of God and men, the man Christ Jesus, where is our blessed Lady? Where are then St. Peter and other saints?

Brusierd's response was to concede Christ as the Supreme Mediator, but argue that though the Scriptures made this point, it was before the saints had died and therefore before their sanction by the church as additional mediators.

Bilney, however, would have none of it, insisting on keeping to Scripture, quoting Jesus in the Gospels saying,

> 'Whatever you ask in my name', that there is no mention of any other name.

This then led to an altercation on the subject of saint worship and the Pope as antichrist. The debate continued, ranging through the teachings of the Church as compared to the teaching of Scripture.

The exchanges continued, with neither giving way, until finally, the matter was concluded with Brusierd accusing Bilney:

> You wrest the Scriptures from the right understanding to a reprobate sense, that I am scarce able to hold mine eyes from tears, hearing with mine ears these words of you. Fare ye well!

Perhaps this last point defines the heart of the debate, indeed of the whole Reformation controversy—the correct understanding of the Scriptures and their ultimate, final authority, 'sola scriptura!' The long-standing view had always been to seek understanding and interpretation through the medium of the Church, whereas for Bilney and others it was directly through the Spirit of the said Scriptures.[1]

Notes

1 All the citations in Chapter 5, can be found in: Foxe, John, *The Acts and Monuments of John Foxe, a new and complete edition, Vol IV,* p. 619–641

6 Bilney on trial

Who shall separate us from the love of Christ? Shall trouble or hardship or persecution or famine or nakedness or danger or sword? (Romans 8:35).

B ilney and Arthur continued their itinerant preaching until they were both arrested. After time in the notorious Tower, on 27 November 1527, they were summoned before an assembly of Church dignitaries headed up by the bishops of both London and Ely. Most alarming of all was the presence of Cardinal Wolsey who would not normally bother himself with such matters.

Summoned before Wolsey

A murky, cold November morning found the two preachers being marched under guard to the Chapter House in Westminster Abbey. Bilney, as he walked into the Abbey head down, was remembering his promise to Wolsey earlier about his preaching. Now he had to face the great man once more. They were quickly ushered into seats in one of the great Abbey's chambers, still under the watchful eyes of guards and officials. Neither man said anything but kept their heads down in silent prayer. A bustle of noise behind them and they were told to rise as the Cardinal with his retinue approached. Looking up, Bilney caught site of the august assembly. There at the very centre, behind a long ornately adorned table, stood the imposing figure of Wolsey. Their eyes briefly met. The Cardinal then looked about him, adjusted his robes, nodded to his

> *colleagues and sat down. All followed his example while minor officials scurried about with books and parchments, loading the table. Bilney's natural fears returned, and he trembled slightly. Looking at the central figure of Wolsey in all his pomp and glory, he would have remembered his last encounter with the Cardinal and his own promise not to preach Lutheran heresy. Casting his mind back to the broken promise and the outspoken preaching in Norfolk, he knew that his attacks on the mother Church would be interpreted as Lutheranism and that now it would be an easy matter to convict him a heretic.*

After the formality of introductions and elaborate prayers, the court commenced with a series of questions put to Bilney. The opening charge was made by Wolsey, who asked Bilney whether he had preached any of the Lutheran teachings, either in private or public, which the Church had specifically condemned, and whether it was true that he had made a promise not to teach or defend such opinions. Bilney's face flushed. He was caught out and had to admit that he had made such an oath. He then tried to defend himself by claiming that the oath was not made under correct judicial proceedings, but in a private interrogation and therefore not binding on his conscience. This was perhaps an unworthy attempt by Bilney to play with words and only served to irritate Wolsey, who then charged Bilney to:

> Answer plainly ... and that he should do it without craft, qualifying or leaving out any part of the truth.[1]

Bilney was forced to affirm an oath designed, no doubt, to

humiliate as much as to correct him. Nothing further was said that morning, only intending to prolong the agony for Bilney. The court was adjourned so that witnesses could be got ready, and the two men were led back into custody.

That afternoon the court was reconvened. Witnesses had been sworn in and prepared when Wolsey decided, at the last minute, to leave the court claiming more urgent matters. The proceedings were again delayed until Wolsey gave permission for the case to be continued in the hands of the bishops, who were to fully investigate the charges and, if found guilty, to hand the two men over to the state for punishment.

It is not clear what the reasons for Wolsey's departure were, but Marcus Loane conjectures that Wolsey may have considered two such troublesome heretics beneath him and taking up too much valuable time.[2] Both defendants were then told to leave the court a while. Bilney sat in a state of confusion, not knowing whether the Cardinal's absence was a good sign or not. Attention was now to turn on Bilney's colleague Thomas Arthur. The main focus with Arthur revolved around his debate with Sir Thomas Moore that the sacrament of the altar was not the very body of Christ. Bilney waited with increasing anxiety while Arthur alone was summoned to answer the charges. With witnesses sworn in, Arthur was cross examined in the light of their statements and, when concluded, sworn to silence and ordered to return.

Letters to Tunstall

Bilney and Arthur were thus confined once more, this time for a period of five days. On receiving news that Cuthbert Tunstall, the

Bishop of London, would now take over the trial, Bilney's heart lightened. He decided he would use his time writing a plea to the Bishop in the hope that he might be more lenient. Although very much an orthodox Catholic, Tunstall was also a Humanist scholar and had struck up a friendship with Erasmus, and thus tended towards leniency.

Encouraged by his reputation for tolerance, Bilney wrote a series of five letters to him. As far as we know, these are the only literary remains of Bilney. Of these, only three were used in the trial. They were translated from Latin and carefully preserved by the chronicler, Foxe.[3]

The first and most significant of these letters was written with clarity and honesty. Bilney, believing in the strength of his testimony to saving grace, retells his conversion experience. It is from this letter that we get most of our insight into Bilney's thinking during his conversion. After a gracious greeting, acknowledging his reader's

Figure 16: Cuthbert Tunstall (also spelt Tonstall) when he was Bishop of Durham

worthy status, Bilney proceeds to defend his action. He claims his innocence and, using a wide range of biblical imagery, accuses his detractors of being nothing more than false teachers. He says that he too was a victim of their ways. Like the woman needing healing, he too had spent his money on worthless physicians until finding Christ:

I now understand they sought rather their own gain, than the salvation of my sick and languishing soul.

He recalls his discovery of the New Testament and the saving words of 1 Timothy 1:15, how it brought light and healing to his soul. He describes how he grew in knowledge of the Word and his own growing desire to reach out to others:

At last, I desired nothing more, than that I, being so comforted by him, might be strengthened by his Holy Spirit and grace from above, that I might teach the wicked his ways.

In his thoroughly transparent way, Bilney shared his testimony with the venerable Bishop in the hope that he too, like Latimer, might be moved and awakened by the touch of the Holy Spirit.

In his second letter, he continues to defend his reputation, arguing that his detractors have said many untrue things about him. He likens them to Malchus who,

having their right ear cut off only bring their left ear to sermons.

He goes on to charge that many of the great and learned do not preach Christ sufficiently, for fear of the offence of the Cross. He then makes a further claim that such men are not truly sent of God, but rather like the thieves and robbers that Christ speaks of in John 10. He draws his long letter to a conclusion with a plea that he might meet in private and appeal to the gracious nature of the Bishop, in the hope that he might not break the 'bruised reed'.

In his third letter, Bilney mostly reinforces his claims against the clergy but finishes with a renewed request for a personal interview, adding that lack of paper prevents him writing further. The request was never granted and Bilney remained five days in confinement before being once more summoned to court.

On 2 December, the Bishops once more assembled and swore in witnesses in preparation for Bilney's cross examination. This done, they recalled Arthur and laid a charge of heresy, consisting of eight articles on his preaching and statements. Three of these he denied flatly but of the others he freely confessed. Arthur then protested and condemned such articles against him before submitting to the inevitable punishment and judgement of the Church.

Bilney questioned

The next day, Bilney was called up—the charges being more wide-ranging and severe. Clearly seen as the chief instigator, he was charged under thirty-four articles![4] These articles covered a wide range of church theology. For Bilney's response to these articles, we are reliant on Foxe's account. Unfortunately, Foxe did not comment on every article, so we can only surmise what Bilney's answers may have been. This becomes difficult to assess when we remember that, while protesting, Bilney was by no means a fully-fledged Reformer, in the sense we understand the term today.

On the first article, he was questioned about Luther as to whether he should be justly condemned, to which Bilney replied in the affirmative. This shows that, while Bilney was moving towards the light, he was still struggling with major teachings of Luther, one of which was the separation from the Catholic Church. There followed a series of statements on the authority of Church Councils, the Pope and the Catholic Church. Again, he affirmed, though questioned the Papal authority saying,

I believe that many of the pope's laws are profitable and necessary, and do prevail unto godliness, neither in any point are repugnant unto the Scriptures, nor by any means are to be abrogate, but of all men to be observed and reverenced. But touching all those laws, I cannot determine: for such as I have not read, I trust notwithstanding they are good also; and as for those that I have read, I did never read them to the end and purpose to reprove them, but, according to my power, to learn and understand them. And as touching the multitude of laws, St. Augustine in his time did much complain; and Gerson also, who marvelled that we could by any means live in safety amongst so many snares of constitutions, when our forefathers, being pure before their fall, could not observe one only precept.[5]

On several points Bilney conceded to the demands; with others there was some deliberation and conditional assent. Some articles were of a minor nature. However, on certain points he was unmoved—among these being the denial of Mary's perpetual virginity and praying to saints. On the subject of the Latin tongue being used in services, Bilney argued from 1 Corinthians 14, that men should be taught in their own tongue and the Masses to be read in English. In fact, he goes on to qualify the rightness of all men having the Scriptures in a language that they can read but adds cautiously that they need faithful pastors to help them understand.

Regarding Indulgences—a hot potato on the continent—he gives a cautious answer:

As they be used, and have too long been, it was better that they should be restrained, than that they should be any longer used as they have been, to the injury of Christ's passion.[6]

It seems Bilney answered with some variety, agreeing in many cases, adding qualifications in some and refuting others. Yet, in the eyes of the court, Bilney had not sufficiently satisfied them and was dismissed until the next day.

As the morning of 4 December dawned, Bilney prepared himself for yet another gruelling examination, suspecting no doubt that all was already lost. This time the questioning largely over, Bilney, standing before the court, was asked to abjure and recant. His simple response was that he would stand to his conscience. Then followed a series of dispositions set out against him, produced by certain witnesses, along with the Articles and his answers. He was once more urged to renounce his convictions. It seems that there was a stalemate and Tunstall, aware of where this was going, tried in vain to change Bilney's mind. At one point, exasperated by his refusal, Tunstall ordered Bilney out of the room to seriously reflect on his position. Bilney only returned a while later, unchanged saying,

> Let justice be done in the name of the Lord.

Tunstall again pressed home the terrible danger Bilney was in but got the reply from Bilney:

> This is the day that the Lord has made. Let us rejoice and be glad in it.

In the end, Tunstall shook his head gravely and consulted the other Bishops around him. Then, fixing his eyes firmly on Bilney, removed his cap—a sign of pending sentence—and solemnly said:

> In nomine Patris et Filii et Spiritus Sancti, Amen: Exurgat Deus et dissipentur inimici ejus. (In the name of the Father and of the Son and of the Holy Spirit Amen. Let God's enemies be scattered.)

Afterwards, he made the sign of the cross on his forehead and chest and addressed Bilney:

> I, by the consent and counsel of my brethren here present, do pronounce thee, Thomas Bilney, who hast been accused of divers articles, to be convicted of heresy; and for the rest of the sentence, we take deliberation till to-morrow.

Bilney was dismissed in a state of despair. His desire to preach the things he had received was unquenchable, yet, also, he wanted to remain a loyal son of the Church. Such was the dilemma faced by the 'little Bilney' as he was escorted off to yet another night in prison.[7]

Notes

1 Foxe, John, *Vol IV*, p. 622
2 Loane, Marcus, p. 20
3 Foxe, John, *Vol IV*, p. 632
4 Foxe, John, p. 623
5 Ibid, p. 625
6 Ibid, p. 626
7 Ibid, pp. 631–632

7 Into darkness

Do not gloat over me, my enemy! Though I have fallen, I will rise.
Though I sit in darkness, the LORD will be my light (Micah 7:8).

Bilney's defence

On a cold morning of 5 December, Bilney prepared once again to return to Chapter House for yet another examination. As he walked the now familiar route, his mind would have been full of foreboding. Taking his accustomed place before the court, he surveyed once more the familiar faces and waited for the inevitable. Once more, he was asked to return to the Church. The appeal no doubt would have appeared so enticing, but Bilney held his ground and remained resolute. Then, summoning strength, he replied that he would not slander the gospel he had faithfully preached. He said he considered himself a true son of the Church and had not separated. He, then, made a plea that witnesses might be called to speak on his behalf. He even went so far as to say that he could find thirty good men who would speak against everyone who had maligned him.

The raised hope was short lived as the Bishop insisted that it was now too late, according to the law, to call further witnesses. Bilney argued against this, using the Apocryphal story of Daniel and Susanna (Then accepted as part of Scripture by the Catholic Church). In the story, Susanna is accused by two elders of adultery. The accusation is false and it is only the intervention of Daniel that forces a retrial and saves Susanna from punishment. So, Bilney argued, he too was entitled to a retrial. His plea was unheeded and he was pressed again to recant. Bilney was, then, given permission to retire to a quiet place where he could consult with his friends until one o'clock.

The afternoon session was much a repetition of the morning, with Bilney begging to be allowed to have witnesses, and again being refused and urged to repent. An impasse now existed.

To be fair to the Bishop, he was doing his utmost to keep Bilney from the inevitable path of the stake. A man not favouring such extremes, he would rather see Bilney return to the fold. Bilney, though resolute, was, on the other hand, weak in body and low in spirits. His mind was in a turmoil and unclear as to what he should do.

In an attempt at breaking the stalemate, Tunstall consulted with his associates. Again, Bilney was recalled and in no uncertain terms was told he was now beyond the law and he must repent. Bilney stood his ground, refusing to recant, but asked permission to meet friends for counsel. Eventually, the Bishop conceded that he might have two nights respite to consult and return for trial on the Saturday 9 o'clock.

Bilney in turmoil

Bilney, alone, paced his cell wringing his hands in anguish. Pausing by a small table he would drop to his knees in prayer, the tears flowing freely. He rose again, strengthened; he would not deny his Saviour. The key in the door turned and two familiar faces appeared: Master Dancaster and Master Farmer. Oh! how good to see them. Yet their faces were strained and pale. They embraced him and wept. First one then the other begged him to recant, to save his life. Bilney recoiled. What was this treachery? He turned away angrily, not wanting to hear them. Both men continued, pleading that he would listen to reason. Bilney sank to the bed and buried his head in his hands. Why were they speaking so? He got up again and asked for silence; they both drew back. Bilney remonstrated with them. He could not recant, not now. He insisted he had to follow his conscience and His Lord and if need be, taking up the cross even to death. He had endured this much; it would soon be over. His friends countered his arguments and begged that he at least listen to them. Bilney apologized, once more sat down and looked deeply into their faces. These were good men who cared for him. Why should he be so harsh with them? Bilney was weak, frightened and confused Should he not at least listen?

Several more friends had now joined. Bishop Tunstall had deliberately allowed this. It was his hope too that Bilney might be persuaded to turn from martyrdom. The case was put to him that he would be throwing his life away to no purpose. There was so much more he could achieve by staying alive to continue the work. He was the first to come to faith among the group and was still needed. His work, surely, was not over.

He looked up at the anxious circle of friends, his will beginning to waver. Who was he to know better than some of his closest friends? As they continued to ply him, Bilney threw his hands up into the air as a sign of submission.

He came around to their reasoning. He would recant. Wylie comments that,

... the desire of saving his life for the service of truth was what caused him to fall. He would deny His Master now, that he might serve him in the future.[1]

It would be easy for us to censure Bilney for this change of heart. It was regrettable, and Bilney would suffer agony of soul for this decision, but we must concede the mitigating circumstances. Bilney was an exceptionally tired man—days of being brought before an august court would have had their toll on his already fragile constitution, having long been austere in his habits, often going without food and sleep. His state of mind after the endless questioning and nights of confinement would certainly have marred his judgement. In addition to fatigue and weakness of body, Bilney would have longed for companionship and comforting words, such that the opportunity of seeing kind faces would have been a joy and great relief. Bilney's disposition was such that he always regarded others' advice better than his own. These were friends he trusted—they meant well but argued from mixed motives. In his confused and tired state of mind, it would be easy for Bilney to see their arguments as wisdom. He, thus, came to the conclusion that what they said made good sense. Neither must we ignore the natural fear he would have, of the prospect of such a path before him that would lead to such a painful, ignoble death.

It is important, also, to remember that these were the formative days of the Reformation. The distinction between the medieval outlook and the reformed view was still blurred. It would be unfair to see Bilney as the counterpart to Luther in pioneering the Reformation. Unlike Luther, Bilney did not see things as clearly. For Luther, once the stand against the indulgences had been made, there was no turning back. He saw clearly that there was going to be an inevitable break with Rome. He also had the protection of German princes—Bilney had none. Bilney not only lacked the clear vision and conviction of Luther, he was, by nature, retiring and conservative. He never saw the full implications of his actions. For Bilney it was more a question of challenging piecemeal abuses and inconsistencies in the Church—not a breaking away.

To be fair to his friends, they too had waited long in the desperate hope that the trial would turn out better. They had watched, agonized and prayed. Then came this opportunity to change his course, to save their beloved friend. Once the heart is set on a certain action, it is an easy matter to pile on the reasons for pursuing that course; such is the deceitfulness of the heart. The very thought of saving Bilney from himself and setting him once more on the path of service must have been a powerful one.

Bilney recants

So it was that Bilney returned once more to the court on 7 December to announce his decision. Yet again he was asked if he would return to the Church and revoke his errors and heresies. Bilney addressed the Bishops saying that, having consulted with his friends, he was now persuaded that he must submit himself and recant, trusting that they would deal gently with him both in his abjuration and penance. He was then given leave to read his abjuration in private before returning to court.

What thoughts may have gone through Bilney's mind as he sat alone and read through the paper before him, we can never know.

His mind at this point seems resolved; it would be in later days that he would plunge into agonizing remorse.

Returning to court, he was again questioned on his decision. Bilney then went through the necessary procedure of publicly reading out his abjuration, recanting and signing the document. He then handed the document over to the Bishop, at which point he was absolved of his heresy by the Bishop. A penance was necessary and this involved two things, a short term of imprisonment and a public confession.

The very next day, Bilney was to go through his public humiliation. He would parade in simple dress through the streets to St Paul's Cross. Head uncovered and with a faggot—a bundle of wood on his shoulder—he would walk through the jeering crowds. No doubt his friends would be there, but the majority, especially the church dignitaries, would rejoice to see such a man brought low and humiliated. There at St Pauls Cross he stood, as Barnes had done nearly two years earlier, to listen to a sermon which would declare the Mother Church's triumph over such heresy, and the reclaiming of a lost soul from the path of destruction. He was then returned to prison where he served a year—a whole year—to reflect on what he had done.

There is no doubt that, for the cause of the Reformation, this was a huge setback. First Barnes, now Bilney had recanted; sadly, they were not the only ones. The registers, at this stage in the Reformation process, are full of such abjurations, which make pitiful and pathetic reading. Part of the reason for this may have been in the relatively mild approach to heresy by men like Wolsey and Tunstall, and the greater opportunity afforded for recantation. A change took place with Sir Thomas More and Bishop Stokesley; then a bloodier revenge took place on those who dared to raise objections. Yet, although burnings were more frequent, it had the unexpected effect of strengthening the cause of the Reformation and inspiring others to join, even though the consequences were far worse.

As Loane has said:

> Death at the stake threw a lustre over the cause for which men died, while public recantation cast a shadow over the truths which had thus been disowned.[2]

Who can imagine the state of mind Bilney was in during those long months in prison? He had much time to reflect and ponder his course of action. There is no information on how Bilney endured these long months—only that he fell into a state of deep despair. Few can have undergone such an experience of darkness. He may have had friends visiting him to seek his comfort, but it seems none could help; he was in the dark night of the soul. So much time alone, no doubt, would have been spent searching the Scriptures for some morsel of hope; yet he believed God's hand was set against him. One can imagine him in his desperation leafing through the Psalms, perhaps hoping to identify with David in one of his crises, but to no avail. We know he must have been in this condition throughout his sentence, for he continues in this same state of mind, even after his release, for another a year! Bilney entered prison in December 1527, after his trial. He may have languished there for about a year before being released either late 1528 or even in early 1529. It was then another long period in 1530 before finally coming to the light in early 1531. This was a very long time of unimaginable misery and we can again only conjecture on the depths he would have plummeted.

It seems that Bilney, once imprisoned and alone with his

thoughts, soon came to realize what he had done and was assailed with crushing guilt. Believing he had spurned God in favour of saving his own skin, he wrestled in agonized remorse. One can only marvel at the grace of God that, during this long time, he did not lose his mind completely. Indeed, God had yet a few more chapters in Bilney's life to write; he would yet emerge the victor.

Notes

1. Wylie, J.A., *History of Protestantism Vol 3*, (Charleston, South Carolina: Nabu Press, 2010), p. 379
2. Loane, Marcus, p. 26

8 To Jerusalem

For I am already being poured out like a drink offering, and the time for my departure is near. I have fought the good fight, I have finished the race, I have kept the faith (2 Timothy 4:6–7).

E ither in late 1528 or early 1529, Bilney finally got his release and returned to Cambridge. He had done his penance, served his sentence and was free once more, but was now a completely changed, broken man. Gone was the spark that once danced across his face as he spoke of the things of God. While glad to be among his friends, he now kept aloof, preferring his own company. For the better part of a whole year, he remained in this state of mind. His Cambridge friends sought desperately to console him but Bilney still would not be comforted. There was growing concern about his mental state of health and he was watched closely by his friends. Latimer mentions this in one of his sermons reflecting on his friend's condition:

> I knew a man myself, Bilney, little Bilney, that blessed martyr of God, who, when he had borne his faggot, and was come again to Cambridge, had such conflicts within himself, (beholding this image of death,) that his friends were afraid to let him be alone. They were fain to be with him day and night, and comfort him as they could, but no comforts would serve. And as for the comfortable places of Scripture, to bring them unto him, it was as though a man should run him through the heart with a sword.[1]

Again, in another sermon preached in Lincoln, Latimer reflects:

Now when the same Bilney came to Cambridge again, a whole year after, he was in such anguish and agony, that nothing did him good, neither eating nor drinking, nor even any other communication of God's word; for he thought that all the whole Scriptures were against him, and sounded to his condemnation: so that I many a time communed with him (for I was familiarly acquainted with him); but all things whatsoever any man could allege to his comfort, seemed to him to make against him.[2]

It is quite clear, from these reflections of his close friend, that Bilney was convinced he had made the wrong decision and was under God's judgement. The light he had found in the Scriptures had gone. No doubt he would have searched diligently but found no help. We need to remember too that Bilney did not have the clear grasp of the fulness of Christian faith as we now know it. He would have still been plagued with visions of a Holy God as seen through the lens of the centuries of the medieval church. Added to this was his unusual retiring and introspective nature.

The light returns

We do not know for certain when Bilney found release, but it seems that, by the persistent coaxing and counsel of his friends, he started to engage once more and to attend the Bible studies. Little by little, Bilney came to terms with what he had done and while still no doubt sad at what he had done, saw afresh that God was also rich in mercy. Over a process of time God again gave him light. After some months of study, a change occurred, and he was again regularly with Latimer and others, reading the Scriptures and visiting the sick. Once more there was the familiar sight of Bilney and Latimer tramping Heretics

Hill. At last, in the goodness of his Saviour, like Peter of old, he was restored and his strength returned.

> Yet for all that afterwards he came again,' said Latimer. 'God endued him with such strength and perfectness of faith, that he not only confessed his faith, the gospel of our Saviour Jesus Christ, but also suffered his body to be burnt for that same gospel's sake, which we now preach in England.[3]

We may conjecture as to why, at this particular point, Bilney changed. Certainly, God's gracious Spirit was at work restoring him. It may also have been the providential timing of God. Marcus Loane makes the point that several events on the wider scene may have had their impact on Bilney. The death of his good friend Stafford, succumbing to a plague caught while on a mercy visit (referred to earlier), would have stirred his soul. Even more significant was the downfall and removal of Cardinal Wolsey. For all his pride and pomp, Wolsey did not have the vindictive nature of his successors. He was far too concerned with carving out his own career, with aspirations even for the Papal seat, while his successor, Sir Thomas More, was a very different stamp. Articulate and perceptive, an able scholar and committed son of the Church, it was his avowed intention to root out all heresy. In a strange way, this turn of events may have helped sharpen Bilney's resolve. Added to this, was the excitement caused by his friend's preaching. Latimer had preached a sermon famously known as the card sermon. Latimer, typical of his way, preached a sermon reflecting the habit of playing cards at Christmas. He preached about Christ's cards, in essence Christ's teaching, as in the Sermon on the Mount, but also directly challenged the teachings of the Church that opposed the truth. His critics were quick to pick this up, sensing also his deliberate attempt to offer the common people the cards of Christ, i.e., an indirect way of stating that the Scriptures should be available to all.[4] He got a swift reply from Buckenham, prior of the Dominican Friars, but this was countered by a second sermon from Latimer. Though these sermons have now gone into the folklore of popular preaching, the

Figure 17: Latimer preaching before Edward VI

point for Bilney and others was the growing significance of the impact of Latimer's preaching on people.

What became evident to Bilney was the changing times. The Church was tightening its grip on dissidents. Tough times were ahead. It is most likely that the change galvanized Bilney back into his old ways. Maybe he sensed his time was nearly up and he wanted to make one final statement of faith.

Jerusalem!

Accordingly, one evening, in 1531, at ten o'clock, he announced to his gathered friends that,

> ... he was going up to Jerusalem and would see them no more.[5]

As his friends sat in stunned silence and gathered their thoughts, they knew exactly what he meant. Like his Saviour, he was going up to 'Jerusalem' to die. He had come through his bitter night of the soul and now, with clear mind, was resolved that he would make 'amends'. For Bilney, this was the only way he could finally salve his conscience and be true to his beloved Saviour who he believed he had spurned. Bilney had been known to waver in the past but now his mind was made up; he was resolute. He knew too, with certainty, that he was signing his own death warrant. There would be no second chance, no recanting this time. As he bade good night to his companions and prepared to pack, he knew he was on a road that would end in death. His friends, too, sensed that there would be no persuading him now—the path to martyrdom was unavoidable. We may censure Bilney for his past inconsistencies but admire his final resolve, to take up his cross and follow his Master. What this meant in practise was a return to itinerant preaching with the certainty of conflict and capture. He would set out for Norwich once more preaching, wherever he could, the gospel of Christ.

Bilney set out, firstly visiting friends privately and confirming them in their faith. He reminded his followers that, though he had set them a poor example, he was now going to show them a better one. Among those he visited was one lady, an anchoress or hermit whom he had helped and led to Christ on his first visit. He now returned to confirm her further in her faith.

Bilney preached publicly wherever he could find a willing congregation. One can only imagine the difference in his preaching! With nothing to hold him in fear, he preached boldly, confessing his own failures, warning them to profit by his example and to beware of the weakness of the flesh. Church or field, he preached passionately the truths he had rejected at his time of weakness.

Working his way through Norfolk, he turned south and made his way towards London. Stopping at Ipswich, he preached not only the gospel, but further denounced errors of Rome, even at one point crying,

> The Lamb of God taketh away the sins of the world. If the bishop of Rome dares say that the blood of St Francis saves, he blasphemes the blood of the Saviour.

He continued:

> To invoke the saints and not Christ is to put the head under the feet and the feet above the head.[6]

Bilney was a marked man and his words were all duly noted and used later as evidence against him. Arriving in Greenwich around the middle of July, he obtained New Testaments and gave them to a Christian named Lawrence Staples for distribution. Bilney then returned to the anchoress in Norwich to deliver literature for her good. This included a copy of *Tyndale's New Testament*, and the *Obedience of the Christian Man*—two books by anyone's standard being enough to condemn a man of heresy. They were indeed to cost his life, for it seems the anchoress, in her genuine joy at receiving such precious gifts, shared them with others—the news eventually leaking out to unfriendly informants.[7]

With the induction of Bishop Stokesley, things began to hot up for Reformers. On 3 March 1531, the Bishop had made a proposal to Convocation, bringing an accusation against Bilney, Latimer and Crome for their heretical teachings in the See (medieval English diocese) of London. Crome was forced to recant but both Bilney and Latimer were now, for the time being, out of reach. This confirms that Bilney had travelled south and had been in that vicinity before returning to Norfolk and then arrested. Latimer had also been in Kent during the mid-summer. One might conjecture whether it was possible that they both met at some point, that being their final meeting. One can only imagine the emotional farewell it would have been, if that had been the case.[8]

Bilney was arrested while in Norwich and brought back to London to be imprisoned in the Tower. During his stay there, he was kindly treated by the under gaoler of the Tower, Mr Philips. He allowed Bilney to engage in conversation with another prisoner, an MP by the name of Mr John Petit, by removing a wooden panel separating them.[9] The comfort, however, was short lived, for Bilney was soon returned to Norwich where he was at the mercy of the blind and aged bishop, Richard Nix, who had received the necessary writ from Thomas More. Nix was known to be hostile to the Reformed teachings and particularly to Tyndale, whose writings had been found in Bilney's possession. Bilney was then charged under the penalty of the law as a lapsed heretic. Foxe comments that,

> … the whole sum of his preaching, had been chiefly against idolatry, invocation of saints, vain worship of images, false trust to men's merits and such other gross points of religion as seemed prejudicial and derogatory to the blood of our Saviour Jesus Christ. As touching the Mass and the Sacrament of the Altar, as he never varied from himself, so likewise he never differed therein from the most gross Catholics.[10]

As his eyes had been open to the Scriptures, so Bilney responded. It was, however, still piecemeal. He rejected certain key teachings of the Church and for these he was charged, but he never renounced the Church or the authority of the Pope.

Meanwhile, a succession of friars and doctors were sent to Bilney in the hope of persuading him and warning him that he was in danger of being damned, body and soul. Of these, a Dr Call was in the end 'somewhat reclaimed to the gospel's side' by Bilney's faithful testimony.[11]

Once the writ arrived, the trial was short and sharp, but before the sentence could be pronounced Bilney made a last-minute appeal to the King as supreme head of the Church. This involved the Mayor of Norwich in deciding whether Bilney be taken out of the Bishop's jurisdiction and into the Kings. But, before the mayor could take action, the appeal was dismissed—perhaps on the grounds that though the King was, in principle, now Head of the Church, he had not been officially confirmed by Parliament. The appeal was to have repercussions at a later date, long after Bilney's death.[12]

Latimer, hearing of his friend's arrest, travelled to London where he preached a sermon urging the judges to be lenient on Bilney and not accept the false reports. He even said that if the Bishop of London accepted the accusations of the enemies of St Paul, 'then good St Paul must have borne a faggot at Paul's Cross'.[13]

Bilney was now at the point of no return but was at peace. He had abjured his former weaknesses and set his heart on the inevitable martyrdom. He was now full of faith and ready to die for his Lord.

Notes

1 Latimer, Hugh, *Sermons by Hugh Latimer, Sometime Bishop of Worcester, Martyr, 1555*, p. 222
2 Ibid, pp51–52

3 Ibid, p. 52

4 Latimer, Hugh, 'Sermons on the Card', *Sermons by Hugh Latimer, Sometime Bishop of Worcester, Martyr, 1555*, pp. 2–16

5 Foxe, John, *Vol IV*, p. 642

6 Merle d'Aubigne, J.H., *The Reformation in England Vol 2*, (Edinburgh: Banner of Truth, 1963), p. 72

7 Merle d'Aubigne, J.H., *The Reformation in England Vol 2*, p. 72

8 Loane, Marcus, *Masters of the English Reformation*, p. 34

9 Merle d'Aubigne, p. 76

10 Foxe, John, *Vol IV*, p. 649

11 Ibid, p. 642

12 Gairdner, James, *Lollardy and the Reformation in England Vol 1*, (Cambridge: The University Press, 2010), p. 401

13 Hannula, Richard M., *Hugh Latimer, Bitesize Biographies*, p. 45

9 Lollards Pit

But now, this is what the LORD says—he who created you, Jacob, he who formed you, Israel: 'Do not fear, for I have redeemed you; I have summoned you by name; you are mine. When You pass through the waters, I will be with you; and when you pass through the rivers, they will not sweep over you. When you walk through the fire, you will not be burned; the flames will not set you ablaze' (Isaiah 43:1–2).

Bilney at peace

The formalities of degrading Bilney as a heretic were carried out before handing him over to the civil authorities, as was the practice with the condemnation of all heretics. Bilney had been placed in the prison of the Guildhall to await his sentence. One of the two sheriffs responsible for his committal was Thomas Necton, who happened to be a friend of Bilney and was sorry to accept him into his custody. He allowed his friends to visit and, while not able to stay his pending execution, he did everything in his power to make Bilney's imprisonment as comfortable as possible. Such was his friendship that he could not bear to be present at the execution.

During his confinement, Bilney was allowed visitors. As they each sought to console him with encouraging words, they were amazed at Bilney's calm repose. He would often repeat the precious words of Isaiah 43:2:

> When you walk through the fire you will not be burned.

One of his friends remarked on his cheerful disposition to which Bilney replied,

I shall soon have unspeakable joy in heaven.

It seems that Bilney's inner turmoil was completely resolved. He was able to eat heartily and one commented on how glad they were to see that he could eat, knowing what pains lay ahead. Bilney responded:

O! I follow the example of the husbandmen of the country, who, having a ruinous house to dwell in, yet bestow cost as long as they may, to hold it up. And so, do I now with this ruinous house of my body, and with God's creatures, in thanks to him, refresh the same as ye see.[1]

Bilney, continued in a resolute frame of mind that evening. In the words of Foxe:

Then, sitting with his said friends in godly talk to their edification, some put him in mind, that though the fire, which he should suffer the next day, should be of great heat unto his body, yet the comfort of God's Spirit should cool it to his everlasting refreshing. At this word the said Thomas Bilney, putting his hand toward the flame of the candle burning before them, (as also he did divers times besides,) and feeling the heat thereof, 'O,' (said he,) 'I feel by experience, and have known it long by philosophy, that fire, by God's ordinance, is naturally hot: but yet I am persuaded by God's holy word, and by the experience of some, spoken of in the same, that in the flame they felt no heat, and in the fire they felt no consumption: and I constantly believe, that howsoever the stubble of this my body shall be wasted by it, yet my soul and spirit shall be purged thereby; a pain for the time, whereon notwithstanding followeth joy unspeakable.' And here he much treated of this place of Scripture, 'Fear not, for I have redeemed thee, and called thee by thy name; thou art mine own. When thou goest through the water I will be with thee, and the strong floods shall not overflow thee. When thou walkest in the fire, it shall not burn thee, and the flame shall not kindle upon thee, for I am the Lord thy God, the Holy One of Israel.'[2]

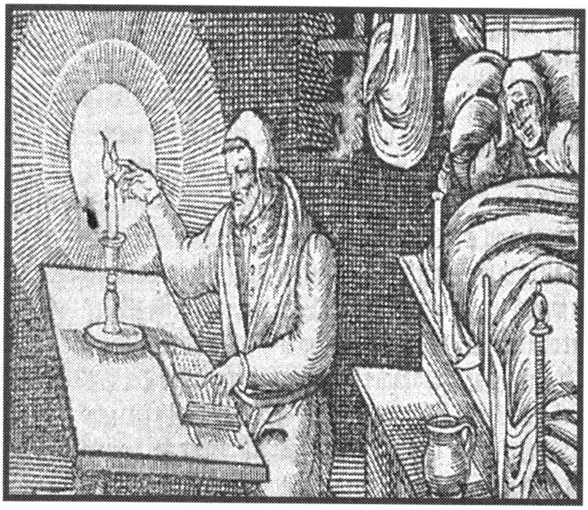

Figure 18: A description of the godly constancy of Thomas Bilney

Some have doubted the story of the *finger in the candle* episode. Yet, recorded as it is in the narrative of Foxe there seems little reason to doubt it, though it has been unfortunately embellished by some later accounts.

As the night drew on, friends reluctantly left. We can only imagine the tears and sorrow as they parted—perhaps reminiscent of Paul's parting from the Ephesian elders, sorrowing that they should see his face no more.

As the last of the voices faded, Bilney found himself finally alone. The candle continued flickering, casting grotesque shadows on the walls of the cell. Empty dishes remained on the table, as Bilney looked up to his God. Perhaps on that cold night there was a chill in the air like that momentous night in his room when he first

> set eyes on the precious words of Scripture. There on the table the book remained. Bilney looked down again and searched its contents. Again, the words of Paul in Timothy were read. Bilney smiled as he saw once more his own young face aglow as his fingers traced the words, 'Chief of Sinners'. So much had happened since those early Cambridge days. Old faces seemed to appear before him; dear Stafford, Thixtill, Lampert, and of course, Latimer. Those long walks over the hills. His preaching days with Thomas Arthur. He continued to flick over the pages: Isaiah 43, a most precious promise. He turned it over with his trembling lips. Yes, he would indeed walk through the fire but his God would be with him as he was long ago with the three witnesses in the fiery furnace of Daniel. That same God would bear him up. He turned his eyes once more to heaven and prayed. That next morning though a fiery trial, he would soon be in the presence of his Saviour, 'Today you will be with me in paradise' (Luke 23:43).

The walk of faith

The following morning, Bilney rose early and gave himself to prayer. Never was prayer sweeter. There was a heavenly touch about the small room. He was in the presence of His Saviour and later that very day would see him with his own eyes. After a simple breakfast he was taken out of the Guildhall, guarded either side by men bearing glaves and halberts. As he stepped out into the daylight, he was met by one friend who would be his only companion for his journey. This was Dr Warner, a Doctor of Divinity, parson of Winterton and long-time friend. As Bilney left the Hall and walked down the steps, he was met by a curious crowd of friends and foes.

One of his friends held out his hand and sought to encourage him to remain constant and prayed that God would enable him to take his death as patiently as he could. Bilney pausing, turned to his friend smiling:

> Ye see when the mariner is entered his ship to sail on the troublous sea, how he for a while is tossed in the billows of the same, but yet, in hope that he shall once come to the quiet haven, he beareth in better comfort the perils which he feeleth: so am I now toward this sailing; and whatsoever storms I shall feel, yet shortly after shall my ship be in the haven, as I doubt not thereof, by the grace of God, desiring you to help me with your prayers to the same effect.[3]

They continued to weave their way through the narrow streets, now crammed with jostling crowds. Bilney, with Dr Warner still at his side, held his nerve and was even able to distribute what money he still had to needy hands, moving in an easterly direction to the final gate leading out of the city, known as Bishop's Gate—then across Bishop's Bridge to the fateful place of execution, known as 'Lollards Pit', after the burnings of earlier Lollards.[4] There, near the banks of the river and under the shadow of St Leonard's Hill was a depression in the land, probably formed by earlier excavations

Figure 19: Bilney being led to Lollards Pit

made to provide material for the cathedral. A growing crowd following the procession would now disperse to take up vantage points for viewing the spectacle. It was the ideal place, a sort of natural amphitheatre surrounded by hills. Of the crowd, most were the morbidly curious. We may shrink back at the horror of such an entertainment but, for the times, it was not so shocking. Some among the throng would have been faithful friends and secret admirers of little Bilney, while others would have taken opportunity to hurl abuse and condemn the unfortunate heretic. Bilney would be the first of many to suffer on English soil as a Reformer. There would be yet many more, especially in the reign of Queen Mary.

That blessed martyr

So Bilney, accompanied by his friend Dr Warner, descended into the pit dressed in simple clothes with hair dishevelled—a diminutive figure. A pile of faggots was being placed around a stake in readiness. Bilney paused and turned to face the crowds and asked if he might have leave to address them. Given permission, according to Foxe, he spoke as follows:

> 'Good people! I am come hither to die, and born I was to live under that condition, naturally to die again; and that ye may testify that I depart out of this present life as a true Christian man, in a right belief towards Almighty God, I will rehearse unto you in a fast faith the articles of my creed,' and then he began to rehearse them in order, as they be in the common Creed, with oft elevating his eyes and hands to Almighty God; and at the article of Christ's incarnation, having a little meditation in himself, and coming to the word 'crucified,' he humbly bowed himself, and made great reverence; and then proceeding in the articles, and coming to these words, 'I believe the

catholic church,' there he paused, and spake these words: 'Good people! I must here confess to have offended the church, in preaching once against the prohibition of the same, at a poor cure belonging to Trinity-hall, in Cambridge, where I was fellow; earnestly entreated thereunto by the curate and other good people of the parish, showing that they had no sermon there of long time before: and so in my conscience moved, I did make a poor collation unto them, and thereby ran into the disobedience of certain authority in the church, by whom I was prohibited; howbeit I trust at the general day, charity, that moved me to this act, shall bear me out at the judgment-seat of God:' and so he proceeded on, without any manner of words of recantation, or charging any man for procuring him to his death.[5]

Bilney then stepped to the pile and removed his gown, handing it to Dr Warner. He knelt down on a little ledge in front of the stake with eyes and hands raised to heaven. He prayed that God would receive his soul, ending with Psalm 143:1–3:

Hear my prayer, O Lord, Give ear to my supplications! Answer me in Your faithfulness, in Your righteousness! And do not enter into judgment with Your servant, for in Your sight no man living is righteous. For the enemy has persecuted my soul; He has crushed my life to the ground; He has made me dwell in dark places, like those who have long been dead.[6]

Rising, he turned to the officers and, seeing they were ready, removed his jacket and doublet. Standing on the ledge he was quickly fastened to the stake by a chain as he said goodbye to his friend Warner, who was by now overcome with tears. Whereupon Bilney leaned towards him smiling and echoing the words of Paul to the Ephesian elders said:

'O Master Doctor! Feed your flock, feed your flock; that when the Lord cometh, he may find you so doing.' And, 'Farewell, good Master Doctor! and pray for me.'[7]

As Warner left, so the friars, doctors and priors, responsible for his sentence, approached, imploring Bilney to speak to the crowd on their behalf. They feared the resentment, generated against them by this deed, might affect their character and in turn, alms giving. A mark of the man's greatness is that, even on the point of death, when those responsible for his trial, fearing the crowd, came to him and urged him so, he consented and with a loud voice said:

> I pray you, good people! Be never the worse to these men for my sake, as though they should be the authors of my death; it was not they.[8]

Foxe, graphically draws the final scene:

Figure 20: Bilney's martyrdom

Then the officers put reeds and faggots about his body, and set fire on the reeds, which made a very great flame, which sparkled and deformed the visor of his face; he holding up his hands, and knocking upon his breast, crying sometimes 'Jesus!' sometimes, 'Credo!' [meaning 'I believe'] which flame was blown away from him by the violence of the wind, which was that day, and two or three days before, notably great; in which it was said, that the fields were marvellously plagued by the loss of corn; and so, for a little pause, he stood without flame, the flame departing and re-coursing thrice ere the wood took strength to be the sharper to consume him; and then he gave up the ghost, and his body, being withered, bowed downward upon the chain. Then one of the officers, with his halberd, smote out the staple in the stake behind him, and suffered his body to fall into the bottom of the fire, laying wood upon it; and so, he was consumed.[9]

Latimer, on hearing the news of his friend, mourned deeply, perhaps wondering if he too would one day share Bilney's fate. He referred to Bilney as 'that blessed martyr'. So ends the story of Thomas Bilney, Scholar, and Martyr for the Faith, once delivered to the Saints.

Notes

1 Foxe, John, *Vol IV*, p. 653
2 Ibid, p. 653
3 Ibid, p. 654
4 Ever after, Lollards Pit remained a place shunned by locals, at one time a tannery, then a rubbish tip, then a playing area. The only memory of those distant days of shame today is the small blue plaque briefly identifying the site as Lollards Pit, attached to the wall of a pub with the same name, in Riverside Road. A plaque remains on the wall commemorating the martyrs.
5 Ibid, pp. 654–655
6 Ibid, p. 655
7. Ibid, p. 655
8 Ibid, p. 655
9 Ibid, p. 655

10 Forgotten!

The most obvious reason for this neglect is the simple lack of information on his life. Nearly all the information we have on Bilney is derived from the original source of the great chronicler, John Foxe. Almost single handedly, Foxe compiled the records of the early struggle. Virtually everything we know about Bilney has come from this source. The only other sources are snippets recorded in sermons and notes of near contemporaries, like his associate, Latimer. This still begs the question, however, as to why those supporting Foxe's analysis have not produced a biography on Bilney. Even in Protestantism's golden age, during Victoria's reign, there is comparatively scant reference to him. So, why the neglect? Some of the reasons may be as follows:

1. Recanting his faith

His initial recanting has stained his character for many. They point to his weak and unstable character—the fact that his 'faith' crumbled when on trial. He failed when it mattered most and this would have impacted greatly on those who looked up to him as a leader. In a word, he denied his Lord. This was a serious matter, and it was regrettable but, as I have tried to show, he was under the most unusual of circumstances. While we cannot excuse him entirely, I do believe there were mitigating circumstances.

Firstly, Bilney was not a natural leader of dissent. In his nature he was conservative and the idea of rebelling against authority and the weight of tradition would have been unthinkable. It took his dramatic conversion to stir this timid man to begin to question the authority. Even then, although clear on the vital theology of salvation, he was still in many ways tied to the authority and tradition of the Church.

Secondly, we cannot overlook the natural fear of martyrdom. To be burnt at the stake was a most brutal form of agonizing death. Bilney would be aware of this and also the certainty that this would be the final outcome for him. Even before this, there was the grueling process of a trial with the questioning and humiliation that would take place. We know that we should endure trials and we have the strength of the Lord but, even so, who would dare say they would not fail as Bilney did?

Thirdly, he had an excessively high opinion of others around him in contrast to his own. This tended to make him undermine his own opinions and exaggerate the views of others—which led to his listening to the advice of well-meaning friends, who turned his mind to recanting.

That Bilney did recant is deeply regrettable, but it should be remembered what incredible pressure he was under from the authorities, his friends and his own fearful state of mind. We must surely accept the man in all his strength and weakness. His knowledge was incomplete, and he still held to some of the errors of Rome. Yet in his humility, he recognized his folly, repented of it, and died a glorious death.

We must be careful how we judge others in their life and faith. The church is made up of incomplete failures, yet, saved by grace. The Bible furnishes important examples in the life of men like Samson, David and Peter. Each man must follow the path assigned and be finally judged by the Lord. When Peter, at the end of John's gospel, asked Jesus about John's future, he got a prompt reply: 'If I want him to remain alive until I return, what is that to you? You must follow me' (John 21:22).

2. Secular bias to the Reformation

The Reformation, while obviously a momentous spiritual revolution under God, was nevertheless part of history and therefore subject to scrutiny by historians. Since Foxe's great classic, the subject of the Reformation has been repeatedly revised by every new generation of historians. This is natural and right as new material becomes available but is also open to varied interpretations. Foxe's work, in particular, has come in for severe criticism which has, in turn, had its impact on the records he has left. With such vital source material undermined, the impact on the memory of men like Bilney is inevitably compromised. It was not until 1955, that a biography was written on Bilney, by Marcus Loane, and even that was only part of a group of men. For a fuller treatment on the historical reliability of John Foxe, please see appendix A

3. Minor role

Another reason for his neglect may be the assumption that he was only a minor character in the great work. To some extent this is true. He did not possess the organizational genius of Cranmer, the preaching prowess of Latimer or the theological astuteness of Ridley, but he played his part. Being of a naturally shy and retiring nature did not help, yet his initial influence as first mover in the Cambridge circle cannot be denied. He influenced many, especially Latimer, and was in many ways the bridge between older Lollard dissent and the newer, Lutheran-influenced movement. Bilney tended to withdraw from the limelight. He would have been far happier to remain in the shadows and among his books. A public calling did not suit him, yet he willingly followed His Master's call as best he could.

4. His right to the title 'Reformer'

Perhaps a more significant reason, though closely allied to the above, would be his standing as a true 'Reformer'. When we examine his life and views, we see much that confuses. He never really left the Mother Church. He was happy to submit to the authority of the Pope and many other significant teachings. He did, however, attack courageously important aspects of the Church's teaching, intercession of saints, abuses of clergy and many other key areas, which were to be taken up by others who followed him. What we see in Bilney is a man groping in the darkness towards the light. Remember, he had no one to mentor him, like others; no books of reference, other than the New Testament; and few in the beginning to encourage him. Other Reformers would benefit from Bilney's start and would see more clearly, but Bilney lit the torch! He acted on what he grasped—principally, the glorious truth of a personal mediator, as declared in the Scriptures: Christ, the One who could meet the deepest need, forgiveness of sins. In the strictest sense Bilney was not a Reformer, more a 'Proto Reformer', carrying the seed of earlier protest on to perhaps more able, clear-sighted men. He nevertheless was the vital linchpin and part of God's great plan in delivering the English Church from the corruption and superstition of Roman Catholicism. The position and limitation of men like Bilney in these early stages of the Reformation can be easily misconstrued from the long-term perspective of the 21st Century!

Positively, why should Bilney be remembered? What does he say to us today?

Firstly, he stands out as a most courageous man, despite his shortcomings. Apart from earlier Lollard burnings, he was the first in the line of many noble martyrs to die for the cause of the Reformation—truths and liberties we now take for granted. Though he faltered, he did in the end make good. He stood resolute in the final hour, despite the temptation to again recant. Some say he deliberately courted martyrdom; this may be so, but it was only to redeem the ground he had lost. He stands and remains a man of heroic faith who would not flinch despite the flames.

Secondly, Bilney stands as a great role model in personal evangelism. As we have seen, he led several notable people to the Lord and influenced many more. His greatest trophy, no doubt, was the mighty preacher and Reformer, Hugh Latimer. There was not a little ingenuity in the way he approached the problem, personifying the words of Jesus to be as 'wise as serpents and harmless as doves'. This serves as a great example and should be an encouragement to us not only to evangelize but to actively seek out specific opportunities and persevere in them as he did. Who knows how many Latimers may be won?

Closely allied to this was the way in which Bilney utilized what he was given. Unlike the man with one talent, he did not bury it, but put it to use to win the man with five talents, Latimer. The great C H Spurgeon was converted under the preaching of an unknown, ill-qualified lay preacher who had a heart for the lost. We may not consider ourselves to be very gifted or able. We may be more of a Bilney, but God has a work for us.

He sets us a further fine example of a man who put his faith into action. So many falter when seeking to do good works in keeping with their confession. Bilney heeded the practical charity of James' letter, 'Faith without works is dead' (James 2:26). Like his Master, 'he went around doing good' (Acts 10:38). The lip and the life were in perfect harmony. Bilney not only preached his faith in Jesus, he lived it out among the sick, the poor and the prisoner.

It is important for us to remember that opposition to the gospel and freedom to express it has not changed since Bilney's time. We live in times where the hard-fought, religious liberties are in increasing danger of being curtailed. We are at the moment on the soft edge of discrimination which could likely increase and turn into persecution. It may never be expressed in such brutality as in Bilney's time, but the essential opposition is there and growing! Bilney and others sought to bring light to dark times and paid the ultimate price.

Finally, despite mistakes and failures, Thomas Bilney was used by God. In turn scholar, evangelist, preacher, martyr. He became the first disciple and evangelist of Reformation times to shed his blood, that England might be freed from idolatry and superstition. He was the light of dawn in England's night of darkness.

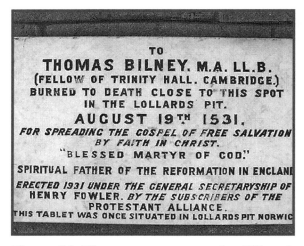

Figure 21: Plaque commemorating Bilney's martyrdom

Appendix A:
In defence of Foxe

After his death, Foxe's *Acts and Monuments* continued to be read and republished, but by the end of the 17th century the work tended to be abbreviated, which gave it a rather sensationalist and graphic focus on punishment and death. This 'tabloid' account was hardly what Foxe intended. By the early 19th century, Foxe's account was used to attack the resurgence of High Church Catholicism by the Oxford Movement, which further damaged its credibility.

Samuel R Maitland, in particular, made it his business to further discredit the historicity and reliability of the *Acts and Monuments*. Maitland, very erudite but somewhat eccentric, had an eclectic career, originally studying for law, then taking holy orders, and eventually turning his attention to whatever took his interest. It seems he was unable to ever settle, often travelling and being conversant in many languages. He disliked Foxe and other evangelicals for what he considered their attacks on Catholicism. Maitland set to work by attacking Foxe's account of the Waldenses and earlier martyrs. There is some justification in this but he used this as a means to totally discredit the whole work as little more than protestant propaganda, concluding that the work was nothing but a tissue of fabrications and distortions.[1] In actual fact, on the period in question, Foxe had a command of the facts which no one has since seriously questioned. For quite some time Foxe's reputation as a credible source suffered. To some degree this has still persisted even into the 21st century, in spite of evidence to the contrary. Yet, the late Professor David Loades, a Tudor specialist, has commented that Maitland, 'deserves to be treated with genuine, but limited respect'.[2]

It was not until J F Mozley published his classic, *John Foxe and His Book*, in 1940, that Foxe's reputation gradually recovered. Among his arguments were the following:

It should be understood that Foxe wrote in a period before constructs of modern history. This needs to be appreciated when assessing him. He was not aware of the dictates of neutrality and objectivity, though it must be seriously questioned whether any historian can be completely objective. He did interpret the facts in his way as all historians do. There are certainly blemishes in his writing, but in no way could he be considered to have been wilfully manipulating the facts.

Foxe had a mass of documentary sources available to him in the form of eyewitness accounts of the events, episcopal registers, reports of trials and other documentary evidence. This actually enhances his work, giving it a higher rate of accuracy than many historians could dream of achieving.[3]

Foxe never claimed to be an historian in the sense that we would use it today but rather a chronicler and recorder of facts as he found them. He presented, says Mozley,

> ... lifelike and vivid pictures of the manners and feelings of the day, full of details that could never have been invented by a forger.[4]

Foxe's method of using his sources 'proclaims the honest man, the sincere seeker after truth.'

Another specialist on Foxe, Thomas S. Freeman, has said, 'current scholarship has formed a more complex and nuanced estimate of the accuracy of *Acts and Monuments* ... Perhaps [Foxe] may be most profitably seen in the same light as a barrister pleading a case for a client, he knows to be innocent and whom he is determined to save. Like the hypothetical barrister, Foxe had to deal with the evidence of what actually happened, evidence that he was rarely in a position to forge. But he would not present facts damaging to his client, and he had the skills that enabled him to arrange the evidence so as to make it conform to what he wanted it to say. Like the barrister, Foxe presents crucial evidence and tells one side of a story which must be heard. But he should never be read uncritically, and his partisan objectives should always be kept in mind.'[5]

While not in entire agreement with this assessment, it is a lot fairer than the harsh treatment Foxe has been previously subjected to.

Historian Patrick Collinson confirmed that Foxe was indeed a worthy scholar and that his text was most reliable. The seminal *The English Reformation* of A. G. Dickens has been described by reviewer Christopher Haigh in 1989 as '... a sophisticated exposition of a story first told by John Foxe.'[6] This surely accredits Foxe a high standard indeed!

In the final analysis, all serious historians of the period have freely used Foxe as part of their data, regardless of their viewpoint, which surely establishes his reputation as a reliable and authoritative source for the Tudor period.

Notes

1. Loades, David, https://www.dhi.ac.uk/foxe/index.php?realm=more&gototyp e=&type=essay&book=essay11
2. https://en.wikipedia.org/wiki/John_Foxe#Historical_reputation

3. Mozley, J. F., *John Foxe and His Book* (London: SPCK, 1940), p. 168

4. Mozley, J. F., *John Foxe and His Book* (London: SPCK, 1940), p. 168

5. https://en.wikipedia.org/wiki/John_Foxe#Historical_reputation

6. https://en.wikipedia.org/wiki/Foxe%27s_Book_of_Martyrs

Appendix B:
Did Bilney recant a second time?

After Bilney's death, it was circulated that he had, in fact, recanted yet again—only this time too late to save his life. This rumour it seems was started by none other than Sir Thomas More.

At the end of his account of Bilney's death, Foxe says this:

> Thus, have ye, good readers! the true history and martyrdom of this good man; that is, of blessed Saint Bilney, (as Master Latimer doth call him,) without any recantation, testified and ratified by the authority above said: by which authority and party being there present and yet alive, it is furthermore constantly affirmed, that Bilney not only did never recant, but also that he never had any such bill, or scrip, or scroll, in his hand to read, either softly or apertly, (openly) as Master More would bear us down. Wherefore, even as ye see Master More deal in this, so ye may trust him in the residue of his other tales, if ye will.[1]

> But here now cometh in Sir Thomas More, trumping in our way with his painted card, and would needs take up this Thomas Bilney from us, and make him a convert after his sect. Thus, these coated cards, though they could not by plain Scriptures convince him, being alive; yet now, after his death, by false play they will make him theirs, whether he will or no. This Sir Thomas More, in his railing preface before his book against Tyndale, doth challenge Bilney to his catholic church, and saith, that not only at the fire, but many days before, both in words and writing, he revoked, abhorred, and detested his heresies before holden. And how is this proved? By three or four mighty

arguments, as big as mill-posts, fetched out of Utopia, from whence thou must know, reader, can come no fictions, but all fine poetry.[2]

Foxe goes into some detail in challenging More's assertion as little more than a fabrication in order to undermine the cause for which Bilney died. He attacks More's four arguments set out in his dialogue against Tyndale.[3] He questions the absence of any documentation, the vagueness of 'many days' and the lack of names. He counters More's claim that Bilney took communion and in every sense returned to the Mother Church. Bilney may well have taken Mass (he had never denied it), though again there is no evidence. Foxe even mocks the suggestion that Bilney spoke so softly at the stake when recanting that no one could hear him.

Furthermore, with no credible evidence available. one must question More's account and motivation. Why would Bilney even consider recanting a second time? It is clear that he suffered unimaginable despair the first time. His tender conscience had been overwhelmed after denying his Lord. He had deliberately set out on the road to martyrdom. He was beyond being saved from the stake. What on earth could he gain from recanting a second time?

The truth is that Bilney, though once wavering yet having paid the price, went on to be the first in a line of martyrs to die for the Reformation truths on English soil.

Notes

1. Foxe, John, *Vol IV,* pp. 655–656
2. Ibid, p. 643
3. Ibid, p. 642–64

List of images

Bibliography

Batley, J. Y., 'On a Reformer's Latin Bible, being an essay on the Adversaria in the Vulgate of Thomas Bilney', (Cambridge: Deighton Bell & Co, 1940).

Dickens, A. G., *The English Reformation* (London and Glasgow: Fontana Paperbacks, 1964).

Edwards, B. H., *God's Outlaw The story of William Tyndale & the English Bible*, (Welwyn Garden City: Evangelical Press, 1976).

Estep, W. R., *Renaissance & Reformation*, (Grand Rapids, Michigan: William B. Erdmans, 1986).

Elton, G. R., *England under the Tudors*, (London & New York: Methuen, 1974).

Evans, G. R., *The Roots of the Reformation*, (Westmont, Illinois: IVP Academic, 2012).

Foxe, John, *The Acts & Monuments of the Church* https://archive.org/details/actsmonumentsofj03foxe

Hannula, Richard M., *Hugh Latimer, Bitesize Biographies*, (Welwyn Garden City: Evangelical Press, 2013).

Lawson, Steven J., *The Daring Mission of William Tyndale*, (Sanford, Florida: Reformation Trust Publishing, 2014).

Loane, Marcus, *Masters of the English Reformation*, (Church Book Room Press, 1954).

MacCulloch, D., *Thomas Cranmer*, (Newhaven & London: Yale University Press, 1996).

Marshall, Peter, *Heretics & Believers: A History of the English Reformation*, (Newhaven & London: Yale University Press, 2017).

Merle d'Aubigne, J. H., *The Reformation in England Vol 1 & 2*, (Edinburgh: Banner of Truth, 1963).